1978

PEOPLES OF THE EARTH

• volume four

Mexico
and # Central
America

THE DANBURY PRESS

(Preceding page)
An Indian woman sells lilies
in the village of San Cristobal
de las Casas — like a million
other women who sell their
pottery and flowers, beans
and herbs, in market places
and streets throughout Mexico
and Central America.

The publishers gratefully acknowledge help from the following organizations:
Royal Anthropological Institute, London
Musée de l'Homme, Paris
International African Institute, London
British Museum, London
Royal Geographical Society, London
Scott Polar Research Institute, Cambridge
Royal Asiatic Society, London
Royal Central Asian Society, London
Pitt-Rivers Museum, Oxford
Horniman Museum, London
Institute of Latin American Studies, London

Editorial Director **Tom Stacey**

Picture Director **Alexander Low**
Executive Editors **Robert Targett**
Katherine Ivens
Art Director **Tom Deas**
Assistant Editor **Elisabeth Meakin**
Project Co-ordinator **Anne Harrison**

Research **Cheryl Moyer**
Charlotte Bruton
Elly Beintema
Philippa Galloway
Claire Waterson
Editorial Assistants **Richard Carlisle**
Rosamund Ellis
Xan Smiley
Design Assistants **Susan Forster**
Richard Kelly
Cartography **Ron Hayward**
Illustrations **Ron McTrusty**

Production **Roger Multon**

PHOTOGRAPHIC CREDITS
Cover – **Alexander Low**, **Burt Glinn** (Magnum from the John Hillelson Agency), **Don McCullin** (Sunday Times). 2, 3 – **John Dominis** (Life Magazine). 12 – **Photo Hetzel** (C. Waterson). 16, 17 – **Burt Glinn** (Magnum from the John Hillelson Agency), **Thomas Hopker** (The John Hillelson Agency), **John Dominis** (Life Magazine), **Dominique Darr**. 20, 21 – **John Bryson** (Rapho New York). 22 through 25 – **Burt Glinn** (Magnum from the John Hillelson Agency). 26, 27 – **John Dominis** (Life Magazine). 28, 29 – **Bruno Barbey** (Magnum from John Hillelson Agency) exc. top rt. **Dan Budnik** (Woodfin Camp Associates). 30 through 33 – **Burt Glinn** (Magnum from the John Hillelson Agency) exc. 32 top lt. – **Thomas Höpker** (The John Hillelson Agency). 34 – Transworld/Observer, **René Burri** (Magnum from the John Hillelson Agency). 35 – **William Albert Allard** (Louis Mercier). 36, 37 – **Wayne Miller** (Magnum from the John Hillelson Agency). 38 – **Inge Morath** (Magnum from the John Hillelson Agency). 39 – **Wayne Miller** (Magnum from the John Hillelson Agency). 40 – **Soulahya** (Camera Press), **Burt Glinn** (Magnum from the John Hillelson Agency). 41 – **Thomas Höpker** (The John Hillelson Agency), **Bruno Barbey** (Magnum from the John Hillelson Agency), **Dominique Darr**. 42 – **Henri Cartier Bresson** (Magnum from the John Hillelson Agency). 43 – **Inge Morath** (Magnum from the John Hillelson Agency). 44 through 51 – **Alexander Low**. 52 through 55 – **Robin Bath**. 56, 57 – **K. Kernberger**. 58, 59 – **Robin Bath** exc. top lt. **Alexander Low**. 60 through 67 – **David Montgomery** (Sunday Times). 68 through 75 – **Ken Heyman**. 76 through 83 – **Burt Glinn** (Magnum from the John Hillelson Agency). 84, 85 – **Robert Cundy**. 86 – **Thomas Höpker** (The John Hillelson Agency). 87 – **Mike Blair**, **Robert Cundy**. 88, 89 – **Robert Cundy** exc. top lt. **Thomas Höpker** (The John Hillelson Agency). 90, 91 – **Thomas Höpker** (The John Hillelson Agency). 92 – **Robert Cundy**. 93 – **Mike Blair**, **Thomas Höpker** (The John Hillelson Agency). 94 through 101 – **Burt Glinn** (Magnum from the John Hillelson Agency). 102 through 104 – Daily Telegraph. 106 through 113 – **Don McCullin** (Sunday Times). 114 through 121 – **Robert Cundy** exc. 118 bot. lt. **Mike Andrews**. 122 through 131 – **Cornell Capa** (Magnum from the John Hillelson Agency) exc. 131 bot. rt. **Frederico Patellani** (Camera Press).

The DANBURY PRESS
a division of GROLIER ENTERPRISES INC.
Publisher
ROBERT B. CLARKE

© 1973 Europa Verlag

Library of Congress Catalog Card No. 72 85614

Printed in Italy by
Arnoldo Mondadori Editore, Verona

Contents

901.9
P421

(title I front)

Supervisory Editor of the Series:
Professor Sir Edward Evans-Pritchard,
Fellow of All Souls, Professor of Social Anthropology,
University of Oxford, 1946-1970,
Chevalier de la Légion d'Honneur

1-18-77 Publisher 8

8 3154

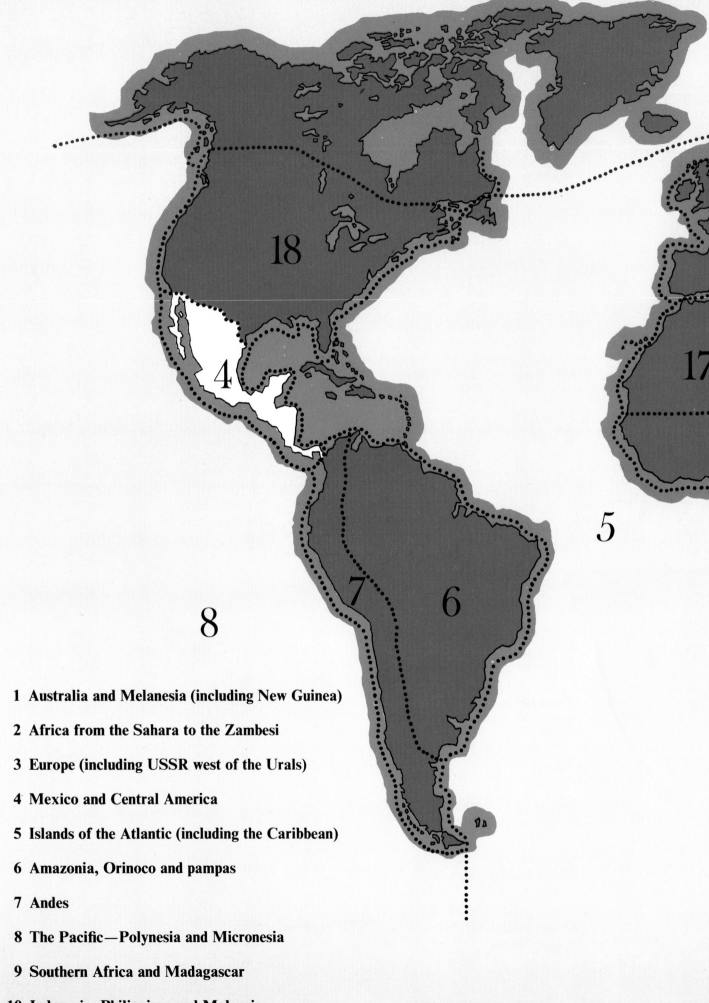

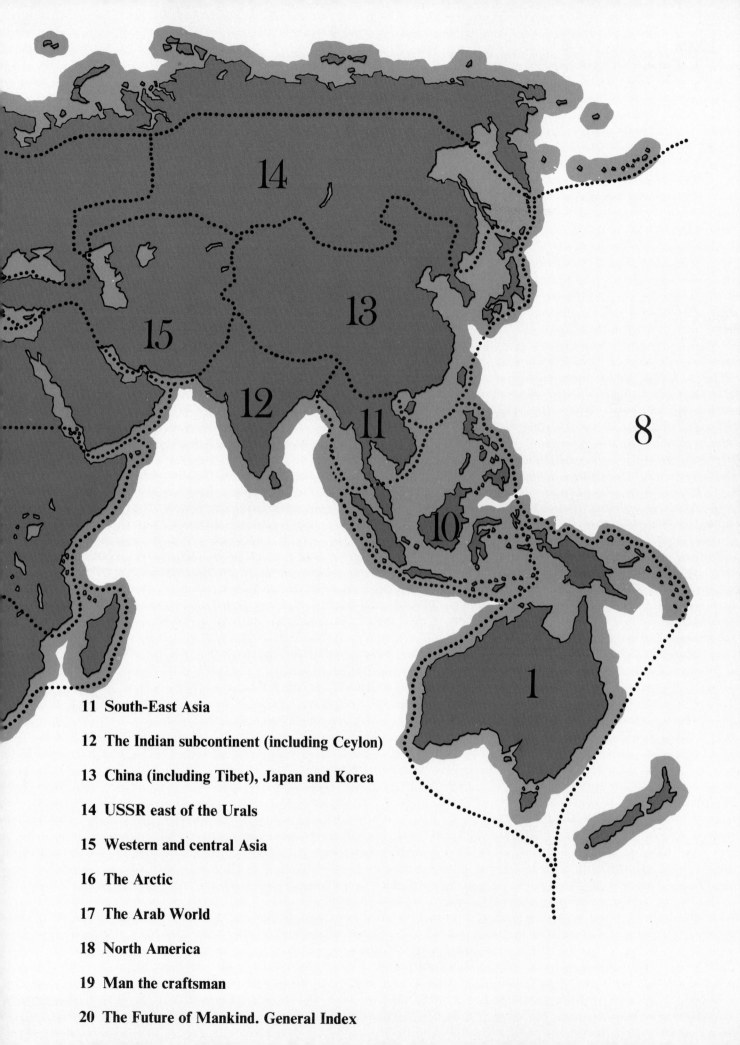

The origins of money

Educated people from countries which used primitive money until recently tend, unless they happen to be ethnologists, to be most reluctant to give information about it. They seek to minimize the important part primitive money may have played in their society and treat the subject with the same embarrassment as they would if one had alluded to recent incidents of cannibalism or human sacrifices or slavery in the society's history.

It can give people quite a jolt to discover that peoples in advanced stages of civilization like the citizens of Ancient Greece and Ancient Rome used primitive money. There is a passage in the *Odyssey* which describes how Eurymachus sought to appease Ulysses by offering him ransom: 'We will each bring a contribution *to the value of twenty oxen* and repay you in bronze and gold.' Evidently Homer did not think it degrading that the Hellenes had used such primitive standards of value and means of payment.

In fact there is nothing primitive, in the sense of being barbarous or backward, in using what we call primitive money. Objects in general demand and in short supply have been used by advanced peoples as a kind of currency throughout the ages. Alternatively, standard products have been used, especially at times when runaway inflation largely demonetized their rapidly depreciating paper moneys which were supposed to be used for reckoning and making payments. Scarcity of coins induced colonists in North America to transact their business with the shell string currencies of the various Indian tribes.

Peter Martyr's observation about the Aztecs' currency: 'Oh blessed money which yieldeth sweete and profitable drinke for mankinde, and preserveth the possessor thereof free from the hellish pestilence of avarice because it cannot be long kept or hid underground' could apply to post-war coffee currency of some of the most highly 'civilized' peoples, even if coffee was not nearly as 'sweet and profitable' as cocoa. We only need to recall not only the coffee standard in countries liberated after World War II but also the cigarette currency in prisoner-of-war camps to see that people who regard themselves as highly civilized resort in certain circumstances to using 'primitive' moneys.

The cocoa bean currency of Mexico before Cortés – usually kept in bags – is an instance of the use of the staple product of a country as a medium of exchange. Cocoa beans continued to be used long after more advanced moneys were introduced and extensively used. An 18th century French traveler, de Menonville, reported that the value of the cocoa beans was kept high by restricting their cultivation. This disinflationary device was also used in the North American colonies and in the West Indies to maintain the value of tobacco and other agricultural products used as currencies. In the Solomon Islands the value of porpoise teeth currency was maintained by religious taboo: hunting porpoises for their tooth-money was only permitted on the occasion of death feasts for priests. According to *Hakluyt's Voyages*, in 1572 a merchant who lived for five years in Spanish Central America wrote to Hakluyt that in Guatemala cocoa 'goeth currently for money in any market or faire, and may buy any flesh, fish, bread or cheese or other things.' Apparently in Guatemala cocoa bean currency was more valuable than in Mexico. Around 1600 an ordinance was issued forbidding the export of cocoa except against payment in coin, presumably to prevent depletion of the combined funds of cocoa and money.

The increasing use of coins following the Spanish Conquest of Central America did not stop the pre-Conquest primitive moneys being used. They came to circulate side by side with Spanish coins. The new rulers got into the habit of using the primitive moneys of the subject people, just as the North American colonists got into the habit of using the currencies of North American Indian tribes, even when trading between themselves. Adopting paper money was no easy matter outside the towns and their immediate vicinity, but all but the most isolated communities gradually became used to it. As in the French African Colonies in the inter-war period, depreciation of paper money resulted from time to time in a lapse into using primitive moneys and even into barter.

Changes of coinage, too, can have their complications. According to Charles Wisdom in 1933 the Guatemalan government wanted to withdraw the small silver peso and replace it with new coins. But the Indian villagers refused to part with their silver peso which they had grown used to. Thereupon the government announced that after a certain date the old coins would become valueless. But the Indians were slow to believe that money could lose its value simply by government decree. They were even more reluctant to realize that the new money had value simply as a result of a government decree.

It is impossible to be up-to-date about the use of primitive moneys if one wants to cover a wide field, although a more specialized approach also has its disadvantages: specialization may give an ethnologist an up-to-date knowledge in a restricted area, but it will not help him to draw any general conclusions.

Imagine, for example, that the Martians have dispatched an ethnologist to Earth to study the monetary system of its inhabitants. He happens to land in Monte Carlo. He would report on his return that white ivory or plastic counters used in the Casino, which also circulate freely outside the Casino, are the principal currency; and that a high percentage of people living in Monte Carlo spend most of their time gambling with those counters in the Casino. His report would differ materially had he landed in, say, Timbuctu, Paris or Vladivostock. The only way in which the Martian ethnologist could acquire reliable knowledge about the monetary systems of mankind would be not to confine his research to Monte Carlo but to acquire evidence from the largest possible number of communities. He could then sift the evidence and try to ascertain what were the common denominators in the widely differing information. It would then emerge that the system in Monte Carlo was a freak system, not at all representative of the use of money by the inhabitants of Earth.

Maize still is, or recently was, used extensively in Central America as a medium of exchange with a fixed value even among fairly advanced communities accustomed to the use of coins. Shortly before World War II the unit among the Chorti Indians in Guatemala was a gourdful of maize, which weighed about a pound and was reckoned to be equivalent to one peso.

Charles Wisdom wrote in 1940 that the Chorti Indians in Guatemala were always ready to accept maize in payment for anything they had to sell, since it was consumed daily and could easily be exchanged for other things: if they could not use it as money they could always eat it. (The same principle presumably applied to the slave currency among Congo cannibals.) Peasants selling their maize in the market place usually bought whatever they needed against payment with maize before selling what was left over against pesos. Their customers usually asked them whether they wanted to be paid in maize or in pesos. Sellers were usually prepared to accept either, though many of them marginally preferred payment in pesos, principally because this money was easier to transport than maize. The monetary use of maize was not confined to the domestic village trade. It was also used in

trade with culturally more sophisticated *ladino* merchants.

Maize money in Guatemala is a characteristic example of the system under which the staple produce or staple food of the community becomes its money. This kind of monetary system has an inflationary bias. The monetary use of the local product tends to keep its value above what it would be if it were only produced for consumption – so the system encourages over-production for monetary purposes. Even if there are no artificial devices to keep up its value – such as were used with cocoa bean currency in Central America – the people who produce the goods promoted to monetary use stand to benefit by the assured permanent demand for their products and by the higher value which results from that demand.

From these examples one is tempted to lay down the rule that primitive communities were in the habit of using their staple produce as money. This is indeed the case with many communities, and there are also historical examples to reinforce the ethnological examples. In Babylonia barley was the staple produce and the principal currency, while in Japan rice until recently was extensively used as money. In Newfoundland the monetary role of dried codfish was even admitted in the Regulation on Fisheries issued in 1825. Fur was the principal currency in Russia and in Canada.

But nothing could illustrate better the danger of inferring general rules from the experience of one community, or even of a large number of communities which happen to resort to the same solution of their monetary problem. It is possible to quote scores, if not hundreds, of instances which indicate that quite the opposite is true, namely that primitive communities were in the habit of using as money an object or material that is scarce in their community. In many parts of Africa salt was – and possibly still is – used as currency because demand always exceeded supply; owners of salt did not find it difficult to induce sellers of goods to accept salt in payment for them. In the Pacific area some islands used rare shells which were very scarce, while others selected shells which were there in such abundance on their beaches that they could be obtained for the effort of gathering them up. When one comes across such contrasts one is inclined to conclude that the only valid rule for the origin of primitive moneys is that there are, in fact, no valid rules.

Writing in 1963, S. Tax suggested that cocoa

beans were used among Indian tribes in Guatemala not only in commercial payments but also for religious purposes. Cocoa beans, he maintained, were regarded as sacred by the Indians. It is one of the innumerable confirmations of Bernhard Laum's theory, expounded with many examples from Homer onward in his book, *Heiliges Geld* about the religious origins of money. However, this theory, like so many others, was inclined to be one-sided. It is just as easy to quote examples that support other theories of the origin of money. Money, one could contend, originated through its ornamental use: or as political payments such as ransom, blood money or fines; or its origin might be as a status symbol – the number of cattle determined the status of East African tribesmen – or as payment of bride price. Nor has the idea of its origin through economic use of certain objects – as a store of wealth, standard of deferred payments, standard of value, and even as a favorite medium of barter – been overlooked. The *potlatch* – the competitive gift exchange system practised by North American Indian tribes by which gifts were grandly bestowed to the less fortunate on the basis that they would be returned with interest – shows that ceremonial and competitive exchanges, by which valuable goods are swopped for valuable prestige, add to the apparently endless list of means by which primitive moneys came into existence in various parts of the world.

European traders easily induced West African tribes to treat bottles of gin or guns which were in great demand as money. Guns even became one of the many abstract units of account in a number of communities: like oxen in Homeric Greece, payment was reckoned in them, but actual payment was made in other objects, the value of which was sometimes fixed in terms of guns, while in other instances it was a matter for negotiation.

Primitive money may or may not have an intrinsic value. According to Bancroft, Mexican Indians used small pieces of cotton cloth for the purchase of goods of small value. There is a 15th century story, quoted by Prescott, about an Aztec emperor who, when he overheard the complaints of poor wood-men, ordered his officers to bring them a quantity of cloth and a generous supply of cocoa.

In the Pacific many objects used for monetary purposes were neither useful nor ornamental and owed their acceptability and their value solely to the assumption that others would accept them in payment for their goods or services. In this respect there seems to be little or no difference between the simple islanders of the Pacific and over-sophisticated finance ministers and central bank governors in western society, who are prepared to accept fictitious book entries called Special Drawing Rights. These Rights are not convertible and nobody is responsible for their value, but they are accepted on the assumption that other governments or central banks would also readily accept them in spite of their lack of intrinsic value.

Then at the other extreme there are many systems in which money must have full intrinsic value to be acceptable. Metals exchange hands by weight. In pre-Conquest Mexico gold dust was one of the media of exchange, and was kept in transparent quills so that recipients could ascertain its quantity: it changed hands according to the size of the quill. Another preconquest metallic currency was copper hatchets each equivalent to 8,000 cocoa beans in the early 16th century. Cortés found pieces of tin circulating in several provinces. Others, too, made reference to T-shaped pieces of tin and copper.

These objects may have had intrinsic value, but their nominal value was possibly in excess of their metallic value. The first historical instance of metallic fiduciary currency – founded on trust or public confidence – was that of the Spartan iron bars introduced by Lycurgus. According to Plutarch these bars were rendered deliberately useless by some metallurgical process by which the iron was made too brittle to be used.

In many instances primitive moneys were used by poor communities which could not afford coinage. In a Maya village, money was so scarce during the inter-war period that it was almost impossible to get change even for such a small coin as 25 cents. Eggs were therefore used for change and for small transactions. Prices for corncake, rice or cocoa among others were quoted in eggs. The same currency was used for the same reason until quite recently in the Outer Hebrides and in some of the Scilly Isles, because the limited amount of modern money in circulation was needed for rents or other payments for which only modern money was accepted.

On the other hand, primitive money has often been used in communities which were by comparison positively wealthy. The extensive use of cattle and goats as currency in East Africa led to the accumulation of vast herds. The result has been over-grazing and land erosion. In a way the tsetse fly acted as nature's balancing influence, because, by keeping down the accumulation of wealth in the form of cattle and goats, it mitigated land erosion. This was one of the reasons why the groundnut scheme of the Attlee (British) government was so ill-advised. To prepare the soil for groundnuts, the bush was uprooted over a vast territory with the result that the tsetse fly was eliminated. While this had certain advantages it did prepare the way for an increase in the number of cattle and goats used for monetary purposes. From this point of view at any rate, the failure of the groundnut scheme was a blessing in disguise.

Although primitive money still holds its own in some societies the number of these societies is rapidly declining. Ethnologists have to penetrate the unexplored interiors of New Guinea or Brazil to discover communities where modern money has not yet succeeded in replacing their primitive moneys. In a much larger number of communities, which are also more accessible, primitive moneys survive, but with their role curtailed. Objects used for monetary purposes tend to decline to the extent to which populations become detribalized. In many communities bride price is still paid wholly or partly in primitive money, and it is still used for cere-monial purposes. But in spite of efforts to keep up old traditions modern money is gaining on primi-tive money. For instance in the Pacific island of Pelew where the incredibly complicated system of multiple bead currencies still – or at any rate until the 1960s – flourishes, young men are increasingly reluctant to accept beads in payment for their goods and services. But then since there is a lack of standardized units in the Pelew system, it is a matter of opinion whether the beads could be con-sidered a currency anyway under any but the loosest definition.

When Margaret Mead revisited the Admiralty Islands in 1953 after an absence of a quarter of a century she found that during and after World War II modern money had penetrated the com-munity of the Manu. But its acceptability as pay-ment for goods and services was no more auto-matic than were dogs' teeth and shell beads in the old days. 'Native money was ineffective in the old system. European money is just as ineffective' she said. By which she meant that in the primitive monetary system of the Manu, as of other com-munities in the Pacific and elsewhere where varied currencies circulated side by side, each kind of currency was accepted only for certain kinds of payments.

There is much evidence that in many communi-ties modern money is used as if it were a new type of primitive money. There are still tribes in which coins are treated as ornaments. To establish the general use of modern money in undeveloped com-munities, it is not sufficient to adopt measures aimed at eliminating or drastically curtailing the use of primitive money. It would be necessary to abolish tribal systems and achieve far-reaching social changes which would not be beneficial to the popu-lation, especially if the changes were enforced too suddenly.

For a long time ethnologists have given little help to the authorities – whether colonial or independent governments – in the difficult task of adapting their communities to the use of modern money in a modern sense.

Following the sudden contract between backward and advanced communities during and since World War II, modern money, modern systems of produc-tion and modern market economy were forced, before they could be prepared for them, on un-developed communities in a matter of years. There were striking anomalies – which gave rise to situ-ations which must surely be interesting to ethno-logists who ought to have thoroughly investigated them. Although in fairness, they were investigated in more recent years in a number of isolated com-munities, and several highly valuable monographs were published as a result, what was, and still is, needed is an adequate summing up of their separate findings.

Is this because economic anthropology, like economic theory, has come to make it a point of honor to keep aloof from real life? Perhaps the root of the trouble is the lack of adequate contact between the two disciplines concerned – ethnology and economics. Broadly speaking, ethnologists do not make an adequate effort to become economists and they do less than nothing to encourage econo-mists to become ethnologists. So while there are a number of economic anthropologists there are very few anthropological economists – which is a dis-tinction with a difference.

The sands are running out as far as primitive currencies are concerned. There are very few com-munities left which still provide an opportunity for field research, except for the purpose of studying the transition from primitive to modern money and the anomalies referred to above. Nevertheless, that task is well worth undertaking.   11

Peoples of Mexico and Central America

When the Spaniards conquered Mexico and Central America in the early 16th century they gave to the varied inhabitants of those lands the general name of 'Indians', as they had already named the peoples of the Indies. And so Columbus' error in thinking that he had reached India has been perpetuated to this day, though the Indians are no longer as they were at the time of the Spanish Conquest.

They were then divided into many kingdoms and tribes. Though all of Mongoloid stock they varied in physical type, language and cultural achievement. There flourished at that time the two great civilizations of the Aztecs and the Maya. These peoples possessed cities and temples of stone and a form of writing that was more advanced than picture representations. Their priests performed complex calculations in the elaboration of their calendar, which was of central importance in their religion. These ancient civilizations were all the more remarkable because they used no metal (except as adornment), no animal power and no wheel. The Aztecs had recently conquered the greater part of the area and held much of its population in resentful subordination. But the political unity of the Maya of Yucatán had already disintegrated when the Spaniards arrived and they were organized in small city-states. Local rivalries and the Indians' awe at the Spaniards' horses and firearms made their resistance ineffective. Within a decade or two almost the whole of Mexico and Central America were under Spanish domination.

At first the Spaniards governed largely through the traditional Indian authorities whom they recognized at the local level, and through the services of certain tribes, notably the Tlaxcalans and Mexicans, who provided them with garrisons to hold the local tribes in check. The Spaniards – only a few thousand among a population of some twenty or thirty millions – could hardly have managed otherwise. But in time the relative numbers of Spaniards and Indians changed and with it the nature of the colonial society itself. The Spanish population increased steadily as more immigrants arrived, while the Indians declined disastrously. Within a hundred years they numbered less than a tenth of their former strength.

The Indians' decline was caused by more than warfare, this crushing of rebellions and the disorganization of the indigenous way of life. New diseases had been introduced from Europe, against which the Indian physique was unable to resist. Whooping-cough, measles and various poxes carried off whole populations. In most places the inhabitants of the lowlands were virtually wiped out by yellow fever (from Africa) and malaria. Sugar, which was the most coveted product of the colony after minerals, grew only in the disease-ridden lowland climate and required much labor. So African slaves, already introduced into the Indies to replace the dying Indians, were imported to work on the plantations. In any case Indian labor was found unsatisfactory in mines and plantations and the colonial legislation repeatedly prohibited the enslavement of Indians who, once credited with souls and decreed capable of becoming good Christians, were made wards of the crown.

The Indians were gathered together into communities *(reducciones)* and closely controlled so that they could be easily converted. They paid tribute in kind and furnished labor to their custodians according to the system of *encomienda*. The missionary orders were intensely active during the 16th century, building convents and teaching the rudiments of Christianity, usually in the vernacular. The indigenous population therefore retained their language and much of their culture, while the Africans who were brought to the mainland from the slave markets of the Indies came as individuals, not in communities, and consequently lost their language and culture. While both Indians and negroes were regarded by the Spaniards as inferior peoples, their status within colonial society was in no way similar.

The Indians were set apart and their rights protected. This was perhaps more a theory than a reality, although the judicial post of 'Defender of the Indians' persisted until the end of the Spanish Empire. Indian communities were maintained and organized on the model of the Spanish municipal institutions. Their nobility was recognized, though only for as long as the colonial administration depended on the local rulers. And the duty of seeing to their spiritual salvation was taken most seriously as this, in view of the jurists, was the justification of the King of Spain's right to conquest. By contrast the negroes were without rights or defenders. The negroes were slaves, whose spiritual salvation was of no concern to their masters. Save for those who escaped to the wilds they lived within the orbit of their conquerors.

In the early period for every ten men who sailed westwards across the Atlantic from Spain only one woman came. The Spanish conquerors' delight in procreation was little inhibited by scruples, and so a mixed Spanish-Indian population very soon outnumbered the pure Spanish; and those of mixed descent were almost entirely integrated into Spanish society. They were however regarded as inferior: they had 'impure blood' at a time when people in the metropolis worried a good deal about the purity of their descent. They were also, in most cases, illegitimate. These people of mixed descent came to form the lower class of Hispanic society into which Indians who became competent in Spanish *(aladinados)* and chose to abandon their natal community were also received. By the 17th century there was a population of Spaniards born in Spain called *gachupines* for whom the chief posts in the administration and the church were reserved; the Spaniards born in the new world called *criollos*, and negroes – both free men and slaves. And there were *castas*. Though the name comes from the same root as 'caste,' it meant in this case the half-castes: the *mestizos* of Indian and Spanish descent,

12

This Zapotec girl weaver comes from a tribe known for its success in Central American commerce, but its love-poetry is famous too.

was forbidden by law. Needless to say, these attempts were unsuccessful and at independence the notion of legal status according to 'race' was finally abolished. After that 'race' was a matter of social status; it was determined by culture and economic position and only roughly corresponded to physical type. The only recognized distinctions were finally white, *mestizo* or Indian.

During the 20th century the distinction between whites and *mestizos* became blurred and society was divided ethnically into people of Hispanic or national culture and Indians – people of Indian culture. In a few places negroes remain ethnically distinct, as for example, the Black Caribs of Guatemala, the negroes of British Honduras (or Belize) or the negro communities of coastal Oaxaca. In most of the country, however, even where there is a high level of African heredity, as in the state of Vera Cruz, there is no consciousness that negroes are socially any different from the rest of the population.

This description of the ethnic mixture of Middle America is incomplete without mention of more recent additions. Chinese coolies were imported into the Isthmus of Tehuantepec to build the transcontinental railroad, though their descendants are no longer distinguished as Chinese. Some time later Jamaican negroes were imported into Panama to help build the Canal. Though African features and dark skins were no novelty in that region, the canal-builders spoke English and were Protestants. They have consequently been the subject of racial tension, not because of their color, but because of their culture and faith. Other races have also been introduced, not as semi-servile labor, but as traders who came of their own volition. Particularly notable are the Chinese on the Pacific between the two isthmuses and the Syrians who are cloth-traders throughout Latin America and who, with the disregard for ethnic precision which has typified the New World ever since Columbus, are called 'Turks.'

Finally it must not be overlooked that a number of educated European immigrants – Spanish, Italian, Scots, Irish, German – came into the area during the 19th and 20th centuries. Though there are no actual racial distinctions as in North America between 'whites' and 'negroes,' there is a clear statistical correlation between high status and pale skin. Since these European immigrants were mostly successful in business and intermarried with the upper class they tended to strengthen this trait. Contrary to the proclaimed ideals of these countries and to the predictions of an earlier hopeful generation of anthropologists this correspondence between ethnic type and social class shows no sign of diminishing in the present age.

The destiny of each Indian people depended on the nature and period of their first encounter with the Spaniards, the resources of their territory and above all the state of their culture. Paradoxically the most civil-

the mulattos of negro and Spanish descent and all the different mixtures derived from the three basic races. These races constituted the Spanish-speaking half of society.

Some attempts were made to control the ethnic status of individuals and to distinguish the mixed population according to the purity with which they were descended from one race or another. At various times intermarriage

ized Indians were the most easily overcome. Agricultural peoples who were attached to their lands and accustomed to the domination of previous empires more promptly adapted to the rule of the Spaniards than the hunters who lived a life of nomadic freedom. The peoples of the central plateaux were all conquered within a few years. The Maya of Yucatan – though they had to be reconquered twenty years after the Spaniards' first occupation – were later successfully baptized and submitted to Spanish rule. But the desert and jungle peoples, the Lacandon of Chiapas or the tribes of northern Mexico who had never been subject to imperial rule, preferred to flee rather than submit to the Spanish; they were still undefeated when the empire ended (1823). As in other parts of the New World, acquiring horses and adopting a pastoral way of life enabled these people who refused to be subdued to continue their resistance.

So it is possible to distinguish between the Indians who were incorporated and baptized, whose culture was modified by direct Spanish intervention in the 16th century, and the Indians who remained free until much later and adopted only those aspects of Spanish culture which suited them. The Lacandon adopted virtually nothing that was Spanish until the 20th century when they first came into peaceful contact with outsiders. These people were able to remain unsubordinated because they occupied territory which inspired no envy from the colonists – territory containing neither land worth cultivating, nor metals worth mining, nor timber worth exploiting; nor, one might add today, were the ruins to attract the archaeologist and, in his wake, the tourist.

The peoples who were conquered and baptized did not, for all that, lose their identity. They still speak a distinct language and there are differences of dialect between each tribe or township. Each community wears a distinct dress which differentiates its members from those of other communities. Much of their clothing is woven by hand on the backstrap loom of preconquest times and certain preconquest details survive, though their clothes are mostly adapted from the Spanish model of a subsequent century.

They interpreted the ideas and institutions that were imposed upon them in their own way, according to their indigenous tradition. Their religion, which has been called 'syncretic,' is a mixture of the 16th century missionaries' teaching and their ancient beliefs. They consider themselves on the whole good Christians – they even sometimes use the word Christian in their own language to mean 'Indian' – but this does not prevent them from believing that each man has as well as his immortal soul, an animal spirit *(nagual* or *tona)*. Some believe that man possesses several animal spirits, who live in the bush, who will die when he dies and whose fate he shares. Their heaven is not a paradisiacal after-life which compensates for the injustices of life on earth, but a simultaneous plane of existence where individuals, in the form of their animal spirits, determine terrestrial events which impose their own justice. Also on this plane are the animal spirits of the Christian saints, the ancestors and the various spirits of nature, the mother of the earth, of the corn and other plants.

From the belief in animal spirits certain early anthropologists devised the notion that there was a religion of 'nagualism', preserved since preconquest times which aimed to overthrow the Spanish domination. Modern research has discovered nothing to justify this supposition. Witchcraft, an integral part of this conception of the world, has an important role in Indian villages, for misfortunes, ill health and death are generally attributed to the evil of others. In most cases witches are not female as was usual in European witchcraft, but male. As in much of the world it is thought that those who can cure can also kill, so that curers are high on the list of those accused of causing unexplained deaths. But in fact any powerful man may be suspected of success by means of witchcraft and at the expense of others. In Indian communities the murder of witches accounts for the high assassination rate.

Religious practice centers on devotion to the saints. Fiestas are celebrated with ritual processions, fireworks and an immoderate quantity of liquor. Great prestige is accorded to those who hold senior posts in the hierarchy of the religious brotherhoods and they are often also involved in civil functions. Religious posts sometimes alternate with posts in the Indian government according to a system called 'the civil-religious hierarchy.' Real power lies not so much in the hands of the current occupants of the posts but of their former occupants, the elders. This is one of the reasons for the Indians' extreme conservatism.

Quite apart from differences between Indians according to their language and culture, they differ by how far they have adopted European ideas and practices. Nevertheless there is no single road of change down which they travel before they can or want to change their ethnic status and join the nation. In many communities Indians can speak Spanish. There are even some in eastern Guatemala who can speak nothing else, yet are still recognized as Indians. Even more frequently the men especially have changed to western dress.

Yet although European dress and speaking Spanish are indispensable for a change of ethnic status, they do not necessarily bring it about. Nor does the one always go with the other. Some communities have changed in one way, some in another, but in the last resort the question of whether or not they are still Indian depends not only upon their own ambitions but also on the verdict of their neighbors. This is not always clearly given. There are communities in transition where the old people still wear Indian dress and speak the Indian language while the young dress in western style and deny knowing any language but Spanish. It has been suggested that this change is simply due to improved communications. But there are still intact Indian communities on the outskirts of cities such as Puebla or Guatemala City and there are others who live on main roads built as long ago as the 18th century.

Since most *mestizos* are descended within the last few generations from an Indian mother, it is only to be expected that the uneducated retain ideas and practices which recall the culture of their forebears: witchcraft and certain rituals involved in agriculture or house-building, for example. However, witchcraft and curing are mainly in the hands of women, not men, and the agricultural rituals are followed only as long as the traditional techniques of growing corn and building are employed. It is not easy to generalize even about the 'baptized' Indians, so varied are they, and so varied are the uses of the term 'Indian.'

In many cases Indians can be seen simply as an indigenous peasantry, but any attempt to explain their existence simply in terms of social class overlooks the fact that *mestizos* commonly live in their vicinity: the *mestizos* are peasants and laborers no better off than the Indians. Moreover in certain areas, notably western Guatemala, Indians who have become educated in Spanish and wealthy as merchants remain Indian. And the claim to be Indian is also often made on purely ideological grounds. The doctrines of the Mexican Revolution exalted the indigenous origins of the people of Mexico as a reaction against foreign influence and an upper class which prided itself on its Spanish descent. To claim to be Indian is therefore to claim descent from the rightful owners of the land. Indian ideology is the product of a certain form of populism. It gave rise to attempts to revive the Nahuatl language among people not socially regarded as Indians. It explains the retention of ritual pronouncements in Indian language among people who no longer use it in any other context.

Indians are difficult to administer in terms of modern legislation, especially when they do not speak the national language. They are usually poor and commonly abused by people who speak Spanish better than they do. They are generally afraid to defend even what rights they are aware of. When they rebel as they have done as recently as 1945, they do so merely to drive out or massacre the non-Indians who live among them so that they can be left to themselves. Various organizations try to help them. Under the impact of the various National Indian Institutes and lay and religious international organizations there is no doubt that the Indians are now changing in many ways. But it is far from certain that they will all lose their Indian identity and be 'integrated' into the modern nation as the governments hope. Once the material disadvantages of being Indian have been removed, they may no longer wish to change.

15

The Mexican soul
as interpreted by Octavio Paz

16

1	2	5	8	11
3	6	9		
4	7	10	12	

1. Mexican *mestizo* woman.
2. Mask at San Miguel festival.
3. A Mexican hat weaver.
4. Watching the bull-fight.
5. A peasant in a city crowd.

6. Plaza singers in Vera Cruz.
7. A girl holds a candle in church. 8. A catholic wedding.
9. Steps of the giant Uxmal pyramid. 10. Indians carrying

reed mats. 11. An Olmec head, 2,500 years old.
12. Tehuantepic women dance in their Sunday finery.

The European considers Mexico to be a country on the margin of universal history, and everything that is distant from the center of his society strikes him as strange and impenetrable. The peasant – remote, conservative, somewhat archaic in his ways of dressing and speaking, fond of expressing himself in traditional modes and formulas – has always had a certain fascination for the urban man. In every country he represents the most ancient and secret element of society. For everyone but himself he embodies the occult, the hidden, that which surrenders itself only with great difficulty; a buried treasure, a seed that sprouts in the bowels of the earth, an ancient wisdom hiding among the folds of the land. . . .

Octavio Paz is Mexico's foremost poet. In his book, *The Labyrinth of Solitude*, he opens the door into Mexico and into the inner, intense and somewhat frightening country of the mind. He writes not only of Mexico but also of what it is like to be Mexican.

Mexico's unhappy frontier with the United States, over which wars have been fought and goods have perpetually been smuggled, is a gulf that separates the psychology and the historical experience of Mexico from both the United States and the rest of the world. The resentment to Latin America as a whole, not least Mexico, is provoked at a superficial level in the juxtaposition of the US's strength and wealth against its own poverty and weakness. More profoundly, this affront lies in what Latin Americans believe to be the inability of technocratic, conforming, Protestant North American culture to *understand* their own more intuitive individualistic, life-embracing culture.

Yet Mexico is like no other country in Latin America. It is more than an emancipated Spanish colony; more than an emergent industrial nation and neighbor of the United States; more than a nation of simple peasants and 'Indians.' Before the Spanish Conquest in the 16th century, there was a Mexican civilization of some sophistication; a civilization which, left in peace, might have evolved just as other western civilizations evolved. But it was not allowed to do so; perhaps the Mexican character was partly responsible. And this is what concerns Paz.

Paz speaks of *the significance of my country's individuality* at a time when *the explosive phase of the revolution* is over. Now Mexico becomes self-conscious, questions its direction and identity. The theme is perhaps political, but in the first instance Paz approaches it from the psychological point of view. He tells of a people solitary and withdrawn, defensive, vulnerable to sentimentality and on their guard against it. All men are ultimately alone, but the Mexican is alone in a special way. *The solitude of the Mexican under the great stone night of the high plateau that is still inhabited by insatiable gods is very different from that of the North American who wanders in an abstract world of machines, fellow citizens* **17**

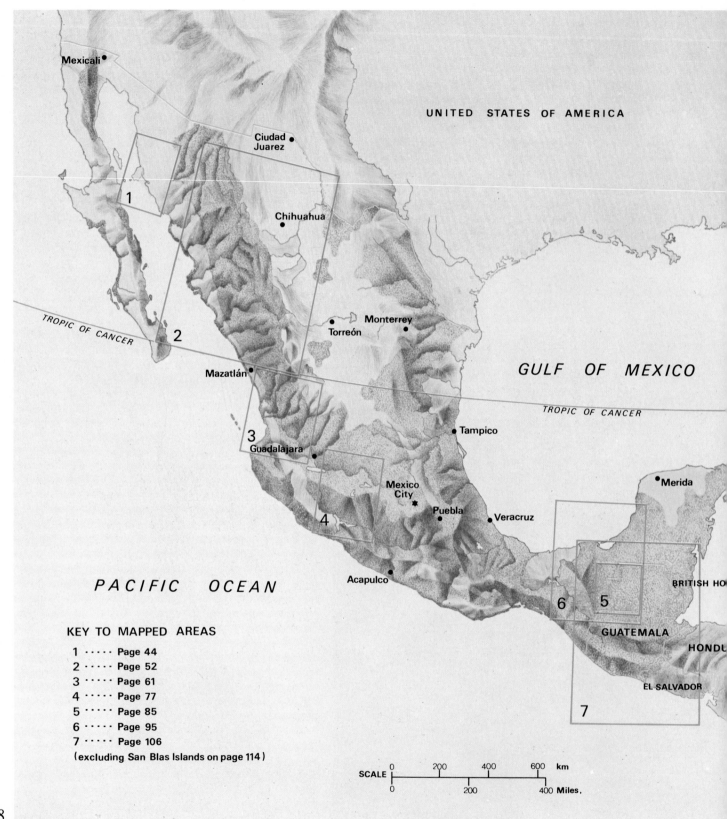

UNITED STATES OF AMERICA

Mexicali

Ciudad Juarez

1

Chihuahua

TROPIC OF CANCER

Monterrey

Torreón

2

GULF OF MEXICO

Mazatlán

TROPIC OF CANCER

Tampico

3

Guadalajara

Merida

Mexico City

Puebla

Veracruz

4

PACIFIC OCEAN

Acapulco

BRITISH HO

6   5

KEY TO MAPPED AREAS

GUATEMALA

HONDU

1 · · · · · Page 44
2 · · · · · Page 52
3 · · · · · Page 61
4 · · · · · Page 77
5 · · · · · Page 85
6 · · · · · Page 95
7 · · · · · Page 106

EL SALVADOR

7

(excluding San Blas Islands on page 114)

SCALE

| 0 | 200 | 400 | 600 km |

| 0 | | 200 | 400 Miles. |

and moral precepts. In the Valley of Mexico, man feels himself suspended between heaven and earth, and he oscillates between contrary powers and forces, and petrified eyes, and devouring mouths. Reality – that is, the world that surrounds us – exists by itself here, has a life of its own, and was not invented by man as it was in the United States. Paz contrasts the North Americans' faith, however self-consciously challenged, in the perfectibility of things and in the general friendliness of the universe, and their disbelief in the reality of death.

One of the most noticeable traits of the Mexican's character is his willingness to contemplate horror: he is even familiar and complacent in his dealings with it. The Mexican character is rooted in the experience of two ancient death-orientated cultures: *The bloody Christs in our village churches, the macabre humor in some of our newspaper headlines, our wakes, our custom of eating skull-shaped cakes and candies on the Day of the Dead, are habits inherited from the Indians and the Spaniards and are now an inseparable part of our being. Our cult of death is also a cult of life, in the same way that love is a hunger for life and a longing for death. Our fondness for self-destruction derives not only from our masochistic tendencies but also from a certain variety of religious emotion.*

Paz contrasts some of the qualities of his countrymen with those of North Americans. He examines what it means to be either Mexican or North American.

The North Americans are credulous and we are believers; they love fairy tales and detective stories and we love myths and legends. The Mexican tells lies because he delights in fantasy, or because he is desperate, or because he wants to rise above the sordid facts of his life; the North American does not tell lies, but he substitutes the social truth for the real truth, which is always disagreeable. We get drunk in order to confess; they get drunk in order to forget. They are optimists and we are nihilists – except that our nihilism is not intellectual but instinctive, and therefore irrefutable. We are suspicious and they are trusting. We are sorrowful and sarcastic and they are happy and full of jokes. North Americans want to understand and we want to contemplate. They are activists and we are quietists; we enjoy our wounds and they enjoy their inventions. They believe in hygiene, health, work and contentment, but perhaps they have never experienced true joy, which is an intoxication, a whirlwind. In the hubbub of a fiesta night our voices explode into brilliant lights, and life and death mingle together, while their vitality becomes a fixed smile that denies old age and death but that changes life to motionless stone.

Paz creates not a set of laws by which Mexicans and Americans may be defined and contrasted, but a perspective, a lens through which the Mexican may be observed in relation to his neighbors. Only in one matter is Paz somewhat dogmatic: *The Mexican, whether young or old,* criollo *or* mestizo *(of either Spanish or Spanish-*

Indian blood), general or labourer or lawyer, seems to me to be a person who shuts himself away to protect himself: his face is a mask. . . . This withdrawal from expressing emotions is rooted in a basic distrust of life and the universe and lies at the heart of the Mexican notion of manhood. To open up, to surrender or to weaken oneself is an abdication of masculine strength. *Resignation is one of our most popular virtues. We admire fortitude in the face of adversity more than the most brilliant triumph.* To resign oneself to fate, to be brave and not give away one's anxiety are the qualities of manhood.

The Mexican likes closed, secure worlds. In politics and in art he favors strict form. Closed worlds and strict form set bounds to privacy, limit its excesses and build walls around the Mexican psyche. Courtesy and formality in daily life allow Mexicans to express themselves, within limits, without the need to resort to inventiveness which is demanded by other, freer societies. And so also the Mexican has a sexual modesty (though quite unlike the fear of the body characteristic of American puritanism) which is really a fear of what his body might reveal about himself. *The Mexican, heir to the great pre-Columbian religions based on nature, is a good deal more pagan than the Spaniard, and does not condemn the natural world. Sexual love is not tinged with grief and horror in Mexico as it is in Spain.* The body is not a cloak, but an essence; modesty is another defense.

The Mexican man defends himself by his reserve and by his withdrawal from worldly emotions. This makes women inferior beings *because, in submitting, they open themselves up anatomically and emotionally. Their inferiority is constitutional and resides in their sex, their submissiveness, which is a wound that never heals.* To compensate for her natural, inevitable openness a woman too has her defenses of privacy and reserve. *Woman should be secretive. She should confront the world with an impassive smile. She should be 'decent' in the face of erotic excitements and 'long-suffering' in the face of adversity. In either event her response is neither instinctive nor personal: it conforms to a general model, and it is the defensive and passive aspects of this model, as in the case of the* macho *(the male) that are emphasized, in a gamut ranging from modesty and 'decency' to stoicism, resignation and impassivity.*

The Mexican considers woman to be an instrument, sometimes of masculine desires, sometimes of the ends assigned to her by morality, society and the law. . . . But the Mexican woman does not altogether fit the role in which she has been cast. *Perhaps she would usually prefer to be treated with less respect (which anyway is only granted to her in public) and with greater freedom and truthfulness; that is, to be treated as a human being rather than a symbol or function. But how can we agree to let her express herself when our whole way of life is a mask designed to hide our intimate feelings?*

The masks are dropped at specially appointed times. **19**

(Over page) At dusk the Mexican prairie is still; cowboys, after round-up, linger a while before riding back to the ranch.

Paz's Mexico

Mexican ranchers can match the cowboys of the Wild West with the lasso. The round-up is hard work, but they all enjoy it.

The four ranching Charros brothers and their cowhands set off in pursuit of wide roaming steers which are brought back for branding.

Our calendar is crowded with fiestas. There are certain days when the whole country, from the most remote villages to the largest cities, prays, shouts, feasts, gets drunk and kills, in honor of the Virgin of Guadeloupe or Benito Juarez. . . . During these days the silent Mexican whistles and shouts, sings, shoots off fireworks, discharges his pistol in the air. He is not simply enjoying himself. He is trying to escape from himself and his customary solitude. The number of these unproductive occasions is possibly remarkable in such a poor country; a cynic might see in their frequency some cause of the country's poverty. But Paz sees it the other way round: *how could a poor Mexican live without the two or three annual fiestas that make up for his poverty and misery? Fiestas are our only luxury. . . .*

The solitary Mexican loves fiestas and public gatherings, any occasion for getting together will serve, any pretext to stop the flow of time and commemorate men and events with festivals and ceremonies. We are a ritual people, and this characteristic enriches both our imaginations and our sensibilities, which are equally sharp and alert. The art of fiesta has been debased almost everywhere else, but not in Mexico. There are few places in the world where it is possible to take part in a spectacle like our great religious

22

At the ranch three men hold a steer with ropes while a fourth, his red-hot iron prepared, brands a steer with the ranch's distinctive mark.

The beautiful cathedral of
San Miguel Allende looks out
over the town. Since the
Aztecs, architecture has
stirred the Mexicans.

In the village of Amantenago
de Valle, Tzeltal Indians work
at traditional coiled clay
pots which will be used to
carry and store water.

fiestas with their violent primary colors, their bizarre costumes and dances, their fireworks and ceremonies, and their inexhaustible welter of surprises: the fruit, candy, toys and other objects sold on these days in the plazas and open-air markets.

The fiesta, Paz suggests, comes close to the ancient notion of sacrifice. It is a squandering of money and energy, pouring out the people's blood onto the altar of waste that protects them from the envy or anger of the gods and other men. *It is also a revolt, a sudden immersion in the formless, in pure being.* All rules and formalities are abrogated; *we throw down our burdens of time and reason.* A fiesta is a ritual death of the

25

Weaving hats is the main work for these Indian men. Women do the heavy work in the fields, tending the rice, maize and beans.

Paz's Mexico

Gently cocooned against its peasant mother's back by a woollen shawl, a child looks out in trusting wonder on a harsh Mexican world.

society and all its conditions, constrictions and defenses, uniting all opposing elements and principles so that there can be a rebirth, with the people emerging *purified and strengthened from this plunge into chaos.* The fiesta simulates revolution, when men kill to bring their country new life.

Mexicans and North Americans are nowhere more different than in their attitudes to death. *Modern death does not have any significance that transcends it or that refers to other values. It is rarely anything more than the inevitable conclusion of a natural process. In a world of facts, death is merely one more fact. But since it is such a disagreeable fact, contrary to all our concepts and to the very meaning of our lives, the philosophy of progress pretends to make it disappear, like a magician palming a coin. Everything in the modern world functions as if death did not exist.* In the religion of the Aztecs, and in the Catholicism which supplanted it, the death of the sacrificial victim and of each individual possessed immense transcendental significance, although before the Spaniards came the individual's salvation was not conditional on his good behavior during this life. *The opposition between life and death was not so absolute to the ancient Mexicans as it is to us. Life extended into death, and vice versa. Death was not the natural end of life but one phase of an infinite cycle. Life, death and resurrection were stages of a cosmic process which repeated itself continuously.* Morality and deserving did not come into it. *Religion and destiny ruled their lives, as morality and freedom rule ours. We live under the sign of liberty, and everything – even Greek fatality and the grace of the theologians – is election and struggle, but for the Aztecs the problem resolved itself into investigating the never-clear will of the gods. Only the gods were free, and only they had the power to choose – and therefore, in a profound sense, to sin.*

The advent of Catholicism only shifted the emphasis in attitudes to death. It did not radically alter its significance. *To the Christian, death is a transition, a somersault between two lives, the temporal and the other-worldly; to the Aztecs it was the profoundest way of participating in the continuous regeneration of the creative forces, which were always in danger of being extinguished if they were not provided with blood, the sacred food. In both systems life and death lack autonomy, are the two sides of a single reality. They are references to the invisible realities.*

In the secular and technological society of today, death lacks meaning for the modern Mexican as for all participants in this society. *But although we do not view death as a transcendence, we have not eliminated it from our daily lives. In New York, in Paris, in London, the word death is not pronounced because it burns the lips. The Mexican, in contrast, is familiar with death, jokes about it, caresses it, sleeps with it, celebrates it; it is one of his favorite toys and his most steadfast love. True, there is perhaps as much fear in his attitude as in that of others, but* 27

Paz's Mexico

In Mexico City families will
— as often as they can afford —
follow mass on Sunday with
lunch in an open-air
restaurant.

at least death is not hidden away: he looks at it face to face, with impatience, disdain or irony. Paz rebukes the hypocrisy of American and European societies which pretend to revere and cherish life, while making a cult of mere abstract violence. A civilization that denies death, he says, must end up by denying life. *When the Mexican kills – for revenge, pleasure, or caprice – he kills a person, a human being. Modern criminals and statesmen do not kill: they abolish. They experiment with beings who have lost their human qualities. . . . Murder is still a relationship in Mexico, and in this sense it has the same liberating significance as the fiesta or the confession. Hence its drama, its poetry and – why not say it? – its grandeur. Through murder we achieve a momentary transcendence.*

But the transcendence is only momentary. The Mexican then as always, retreats into himself. *Our indifference hides life behind a death mask; our wild shout rips off this mask and shoots into the sky, where it swells, explodes, and falls back in silence and defeat.* And he sees in his own people something that might be called defeatism, and understood in terms of the servant mentality. *Slaves, servants and submerged races always wear a mask, whether smiling or sullen. Only when they are alone, during the great moment of life, do they dare to show themselves as they really are. All their relationships are poisoned by fear and suspicion: fear of the master and suspicion of their equals.* This fear of the master is

possibly the inheritance of the Mexican colonial experience. *The situation that prevailed during the colonial period would thus be the source of our closed, unstable attitude. Our history as an independent nation would contribute to perpetuating and strengthening this servant psychology, for we have not succeeded in overcoming the misery of the common people and our exasperating social differences, despite a century and a half of struggle and constitutional experience. The use of violence as a dialectical resource, the abuse of authority by the powerful (a vice that has not disappeared) and, finally, the scepticism and resignation of the people – all of these more visible today than ever before, due to our successive post-revolution disillusionments – would complete the historical explication.*

But Paz finds this interpretation of the national character too simple. *The habitual reactions of the Mexican are not limited to a single class, race or isolated group in an inferior position. The wealthy classes also shut themselves away from the exterior world, and lacerate themselves whenever they open out.* The relationships between the Mexican and withdrawn oppressed people is only one of analogy. *Servants, slaves or races victimized by an outside power (the North American negro, for example) struggle against a concrete reality. We, however, struggle with imaginary entities, with vestiges of the past or self-engendered phantasms. . . . Everything that makes*

28

At the Oaxaca Saturday market
as many as 50 varieties of
chili peppers are sold. The
traders all arrive on the
Friday evening to set up stalls.

29

Ancient but treasured, this
automobile will (with luck)
carry this family to Quatorce
where they attend the
festival of San Miguel.

(Over page) At the Palace of
Chapultapec a mural awaits
completion by the painter
Sigueiros. His art evolved
from ancient Mexican forms.

Mexico City has had a modern
uninhibited architecture since
the 1930s. Buildings on stilts
and glass facades came here
before they came to the US.

This ornate but demure room
is in a wealthy family's
house. Once it was part of
a working *hacienda*; now it
is used only in vacations.

*up the present-day Mexican, as we have seen, can be
reduced to this: the Mexican does not want or does not
dare to be himself.*

For this reason perhaps the Mexican fights. His life
is a combat, a defensive aggression. Paz examines this
aspect of the Mexican character in terms of the usage
and implications of one word, impolite but not strictly
obscene nor of literally sexual meaning. This is the verb
chingar, which comes from the Aztec; it is used in many
senses, but *in this plurality of meanings the ultimate
meaning always contains the idea of aggression, whether
it is the simple act of molesting, pricking or censuring, or
the violent act of wounding or killing. The verb denotes
violence, an emergence from oneself to penetrate another
by force. It also means to injure, to lacerate, to violate –
bodies, souls, objects – and to destroy. . . . The word has
sexual connotations but it is not a synonym for the sexual
act: one may* chingar *a woman without actually possessing
her. . . . The person who suffers this action is passive, inert
and open, in contrast to the active, aggressive and closed
person who inflicts it. The* chingón *is the* macho, *the male;
he rips open the* chingada, *the female, who is pure passivity,*

In art and theater, Mexicans
favor strict form. The
starring actor in this scene
of a play, not only wrote it
but also directed it.

defenseless against the exterior world.

Chingar is a word never used casually in public, but only at moments of stress. When Mexican passions boil over, Paz tells us, they use the language of violence. When a Spaniard goes beyond the limits of respectable conversation, he tends to use blasphemous language: the Mexican turns to cruelty and sadism, and his notion of maleness and power almost always reveals itself as a capacity for wounding, humiliating, annihilating. Even fatherhood is invoked in this sense. When one Mexican says to another 'I am your father' there is no suggestion of affection or kindly guidance. Humiliation is implied and intended. *Its real meaning is no different from that of the verb* chingar *and its derivatives. The* macho *is the* gran chingón.

For Paz the word is closely related to his country's history. *It is impossible not to notice the resemblance between the figure of the* macho *and that of the Spanish conquistador. This is the model – more mythical than real – that determines the images the Mexican people form of men in power:* caciques, *feudal lords,* hacienda *owners, politicians, generals, captains of industry. They are all* machos, chingones.

Paz, of course, relates Mexican psychology, Mexican *machismo*, to his people's history. Despite the vital significance of the pre-Cortesian period, the Conquest, the colonial period, the achievement of independence, the revolution and the stormy events of this century, the dominant image is that of one country (the US in the north) being taken over by men of Enlightenment, with the other (to the south) being taken over by men of the Middle Ages. The Spaniards brought their own kind of Catholicism when it was declining and on the defensive elsewhere; similarly, they caused feudalism to survive in Mexico when it was already becoming a memory in Europe.

The modern world cannot afford to be superior about feudalism, which gave men something which they need and do not get from unstructured modern societies – a sense of belonging. Paz is a man of the left, a cautious and qualified Marxist, yet deeply respectful towards the Church and nostalgic for the more organic societies of the past. He is clearly a patriotic, devoted Mexican, yet makes no attempt in his poetic study of his people to idealize them. The greatest obstacle to the Mexican's progress in modern society is, Paz believes, his sense of inferiority. Mexicans who have migrated to North America 'feel ashamed of their origin' and remain peculiarly separate from the rest of the society. *What distinguishes them, I think, is their furtive, restless air: they act like persons who are wearing disguises, who are afraid of the stranger's look because it could strip them and leave them stark naked. When you talk to them you observe that their sensibilities are like a pendulum that has lost its reason and swings violently and erratically back and forth.* Mexican self-consciousness is like that

Paz's Mexico

Some entertainments in the
border town of Tijuana are
quite harmless: a zebra ride,
and a snapshot to take home.
Others are less innocent.

of the adolescent; although it may often be destructive,
it is a necessary stage in his development.

Paz extends the analogy of Mexico as an adolescent in
the modern political society of nations. *The adolescent
cannot forget himself – when he succeeds he is no longer an
adolescent – and we cannot escape the necessity of
questioning and contemplating ourselves.* He examines
his own motives for writing at such length on the
'dubious originality of our character': but he is himself a
Mexican and though he may be more gifted than many
of his compatriots, his work reflects their most funda-
mental preoccupations. *Despite the often illusory nature
of essays on the psychology of a nation, it seems to me
there is something revealing in the insistence with which a
people will question itself during certain periods of its
growth. To become aware of our history is to become
aware of our singularity. It is a moment of reflective
repose before we devote ourselves again to action.*

Now that the colonial and revolutionary days are
over, now that the great powers are less great and less
dominant, Paz suspects that Mexico like other less
'developed' nations will be able to find an identity and a
future and to spread its wings.

34

Mexican people in Tijuana may
cry 'Welcome amigos', put on
garish fiestas or run strip
shows; but many businesses
are owned by Americanos.

Divorces are no more difficult
to obtain than narcotics; both
are on sale openly. Mexicans
call Tijuana *paso del mundo*
— the gateway to the world.

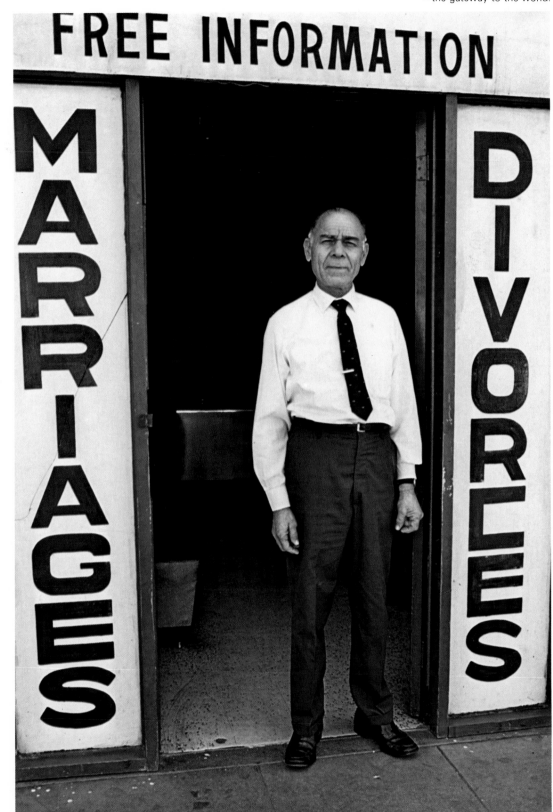

35

The Mexican view of Christ

Besides caring for the
spiritual needs of 10,000
parishioners Father Salazar's
farming expertise is of
practical help to rural Mexico.

When Cortés arrived in Mexico, he was struck by the fanatic devotion and discipline of the Indian priesthood. He wrote at once to the Emperor, asking him to send a group of friars who, by their example and by their austerity, would edify the Indians. The Franciscans were chosen for these qualities and for their superior education, as most of them had been educated at Salamanca or the Sorbonne. Friar Pedro de Gante, related to the Emperor, and who had studied in Louvain, was among them. In any century those first monks would have been considered as having outstanding minds. They arrived in 1523, three years before the Dominicans, and eight years before the Augustinians. They immediately started to build in the most important parts of the Valley of Mexico and Puebla. The principal Dominican and Augustianian centers, such as Amecameca and Acolman, were originally founded by the Franciscan Friars.

The first Franciscans were also fortunate enough to have as a leader Friar Martin de Valencia, one of the most remarkable men of his time. Martin de Valencia, devoted as he was to the contemplation of the Figure on the Cross, gave a continual example of discipline and penance.

No figure could fit so well into the desolate landscape of Mexico. The Passion is logical in a land where the appeal of loneliness and the suffering of man were commonplace. Moreover, the tradition of penance, self-sacrifice and fatalism made the Mexicans perfect interpreters of agony. The emblem of the Cross was planted in this soil and became a part of it, as the Man who died on it became part of the nation's soul.

It seems that this agonizingly human Christ is living His Death in an act that does not foresee the Resurrection. The Christian mind is anchored by the tradition of Easter Sunday. A believer lives through Good Friday in a shamefaced 'let's-get-it-over-quickly' sort of way. He is certain that in two days the problem will have been solved.

But, did Christ feel this way? The Mexican Indians certainly did not. Their tragic interpretation of the agony of Christ seems to have been one of the most impressive outlets for the expression of their art. The little silver and gold ornaments, the *milagros* or thanksgiving offerings with which the bloody images are covered, testify to generations of sufferings and devotion.

Hidden away in little villages all over Mexico are the images of four centuries of Christ: black Christs, made for the brotherhoods of slaves; Asiatic ivory Christs, some seated, some standing, at the scourging post, some carrying the cross, some in big, carved coffins. Most of the earliest figures, dating from the 16th century, are either seated or tied to the scourging post. The crucifixion scene itself was not allowed in the churches until the end of the 17th century because the missionaries discovered that the Indians had added this form of sacrifice to the many others they previously possessed.

37

Mexican view of Christ

Except for a very few crucifixes, brought directly from Spain after the Conquest and kept mostly in cloisters, there are no such images dating from the early period. Statues of the scourging and also of the dead Christ were allowed, but not the representation of the manner in which he died.

Making images on a large scale began in 1528. Motolinia states that the crops had been ruined by a heavy rainfall, and the Friars arranged for a procession to pray for the cessation of the rains. The result of this was so successful that the Indians immediately started to make crosses, as well as images of the saints and ornaments for use on future occasions. At the same time they began making their professional platforms of gold and feathers and lovely candles. These are still made today, but the intricate, lacy decorations formerly made with feathers are now in wax. Perhaps the modern floats used in today's processions are descendants of the beautiful old platforms.

Whole groups of Indians may have been involved in making these images. They were generally encouraged by Friars, who were the only ones apparently able to understand the misery and humiliation of the conquered nation. The obsession with death and its plurality was engrained in the Indian; the list of scourges that swept the country after the Conquest placed the overseers of the conqueror's land in the fourth place, and the gold mines in the sixth. It was against these two scourges in particular that the Friars concentrated their efforts.

Saint Ignacio de Loyola has said that to 'relive the Passion of Christ in all its horror, and experience it in one's own body is the path that leads to salvation'. Nobody understood this better than the Mexican Indian, with his long tradition of self-immolation, associated with Quetzalcoatl, the feathered serpent and one of the most venerated gods of the Mexican pantheon. Everything in the life of the Indians during the pre-Columbian period depended on the gods. Even the date of a man's birth decided his destiny, and there was nothing to be done that could modify it other than to propitiate the gods on whom all depended. No amount of good works or of devotion, according to the tenets of the old religion, was likely to lead to happiness in the next world. All the Indian's sacrifices, whether of himself or of others, were intended to keep this present world from destruction. The old gods were implacable, relentless beings, who had to be appeased with rivers of blood.

Christianity brought the Indians hope through the compassion of a merciful God. However, the roots of the old belief grew deeply. Many of the earliest figures of Christ, as for example that of the Reclining Christ of Sacromonte, in Amecameca, are simply the physical transposition of a former god, wisely accepted by the Friars. This is nothing more than the religious phenomenon today called syncretism in which the forms of an earlier religion are fused into a new one. There is, though,

At the shrine of Guadalupe north of Mexico City, Indians shuffle on their knees to the annual service commemorating the Virgin's revelation.

38

At a wedding in Father
Salazar's tiny parish church
at Tlachichilco, bride and
bridegroom kneel together
bound by symbolic cords.

an important difference. The suffering face of Christ does not come from previous gods who evidently did not suffer. It is more probably that of the Indians whom the Friars tried to protect. It was this anguished countenance that offered the only hope to a devoutly religious people, whose own gods and rulers had been destroyed.

It is easy to identify in this face the superimposition of Christianity on the particularly ruthless and well-defined religion of the previous culture. The artist is never a simple witness, he is a participant. He depicts, as he feels it, the agony of man. The result is a statue which portrays an entire people suffering with and through its God. However, the imminence of death and its terrors finishes by becoming a habit. A horrifying skull becomes, in the process of time, a sweet eaten on the Day of the Dead, in memory of the departed. It is in between these two extremes that the fantastic conception of the Mexican Christ is to be found.

There are so many statues that one feels that every artist in Mexico tried to identify himself in one of these figures. It is believed, for example, that the face of Friar Martin de Valencia served as a model for the face of Christ. Even the substance in which the images were made helped the Indian to find himself in his past. It was the same orchid paste, with maize and cotton, of which the old idols had been made. After his conversion a formerly pagan priest gave the secret of its manufacture to the Bishop of Michoacan in 1565. It was he also who started the workshops that produced the material.

The complicated technique of image-making is described by Cali in his *Art of the Conquistadores*: 'First, an artist carved the wood to the required shape, gesture and expression; details of the face and limbs, and folds in the robes were carved in the softer materials covering the wood. Finally, the face, arms, hands, knees, feet and sometimes the whole body, were coated with a pigment simulating flesh, on which veins, wrinkles and wounds were painted in the minutest detail. This technique of polychrome was one in which the Indians excelled.'

The results were astounding. These shattered human faces peer out from centuries of dust all over the country, and there is a link between them. The terrifying dead Christ, dating from the 18th century in the Cathedral of Puebla, seems to be staring at the 19th century scene of Purgatory in Querétaro. The sad loveliness of the weeping Christ of Tetela del Volcán in the Central

Plateau finds an echo in Atotonilco de Allende in the north where a rococo Saint Peter clasps his keys as the cock crows. The crossed hands of the 18th century Lord of the Shells in Tulyehualco near Mexico City follows the magnificent shell design of the 16th century ceiling near Guanajuato. Thus, all Mexico is bound in a faith that remains constant in spirit and in form through the centuries. The artists are different, but the soul and the skill are the same.

One of the striking aspects of Mexican interpretation of the Passion is its quality of dignity. There is no contortion of the body, or the arms and legs in these seated, pensive Christs. The eyes are the revealing feature, turned inwards, concentrating on an interior vision, as the head rests quietly on the hand.

Throughout the years, the Mexican people have tried to protect this dignity. A satin cushion is an elbow rest on a broken knee. A coat of fine silk or damask hides the wounds. Lace ruffles fall over the torn hand. In many cases the crown of thorns has been transformed into the splendid silver or gold crown with triple rays, symbolizing the Trinity; or even into the fan-shaped crown of glory in which precious stones are set, to represent the seven instruments of Passion.

Though mercy exists, horror remains. Christ has been scourged at the post with the prickly thorns of the cactus, and on the face of every image the gaping wound of treachery, the kiss of Judas, is to be seen. No other country has portrayed treachery in such a chilling form.

The life-like quality of the images is unique. They seem to be thinking aloud. From the little Lord of Patience, in San Francisco Acatepec, with his pathetic 'Remember that they hated me first', through the powerful black Lord or Mercy, made for the brotherhood of slaves, whose 'I thirst' can be heard clearly, to the figure of the Father, holding his dead son on His knees, the words of the Gospels are being constantly repeated. In their interpretation of the Passion, the Mexican Indians are a link between two widely different religions and cultures. The tender Christ and the relentless former gods are joined by the sacred blood of sacrifice. The Indian world was ruled by destiny. Christ broke its chains and brought grace in its stead.

Friar Pedro de Gante had so wonderful an understanding with his Indian flock that shortly before his death, he wrote to the Emperor and asked him to send a

It is the agony of Christ
that Mexicans emphasize.
Mary weeps beside the figure
of Jesus under the Cross
during an Easter procession.

The impact of Spanish culture
on Indian produced the
brilliant *churrigueresco*
style, as in the church
at Cholula near Puebla.

Crucifixion (without nails)
is re-enacted in parts of
rural Mexico; but as this
man with a burden of thorns
shows, the chastisement is real.

During the Easter procession
some religious fanatics carry
crosses and ropes for self-
chastisement during the
enactment of Christ's suffering.

41

Burdened with a crucifix and
crowned with a golden crown,
a man marches to the glory of
Christ's resurrection
on Easter Sunday.

Mexican view of Christ

Candles and pictures are sold outside the cathedral at Zocalo. The clergy were stripped of their wealth during the bitter revolution.

Ancient Egyptians were not alone in mummifying their dead. At Guanajuato three mummies testify to the continuing practice in Mexico.

few Flemish priests to Mexico. In this way, he said, 'when I die, the Indians will not realize quite so much that I am no longer here.'

Friar Martin de Valencia was able to transfer the Indians' obsession with their own gods and rites to the Face of Christ. It was he who originated the legend of the Christ of Sacromonte, and he spent the last years of his life in Amecameca, near the cave where the famous image now rests. It is said that he had the same love for animals which distinguished Saint Francis, and that the birds would gather in the trees to sing to him. Since his death the grove near the cave has been strangely silent. During the last four hundred years the birds have sung elsewhere.

The Franciscans were also excellent linguists. Determined to protect the Indians from Spanish exploitation the Friars did not teach the Indians Spanish, but taught them instead in their own main language, Nahuatl. As this was not the language of all the Indians the Friars had to learn many other languages. Friar Andrés de Olmos, for example, was able to preach in ten different dialects, and most of his confrères spoke three or four.

Between the years 1524 and 1572, the Franciscans published over eighty books in Nahuatl, Tarascan, Otomi, and other languages. Friars who were unable to learn the dialects taught by means of a kind of Punch and Judy show. They would make puppets and enact scenes with them, giving the Indians a terrifying idea of what would be sure to happen to them in hell, and a charming idea of what might happen to them in heaven.

The far-sighted policy of the Franciscans, who wanted to make the Indians Christians, but not Spaniards, endeared the Friars to the Indians. However, the Spaniards accused them of disloyalty. Possibly, had it not been for the Friars, the Indians would have been exterminated, as had been the case on the Islands.

Later, under Philip II, when the clergy lost its initial humility, the attitude of the Indians also changed. But even in present-day Mexico, a glance at a map of the zones of influence of the different religious orders shows that no massacres occurred in the 20th century in a zone that was, in the 16th century, under Franciscan influence.

From an artistic point of view, the systematic destruction of temples, idols and codices by the religious orders, is distressing. Philip II came to the Spanish throne in the middle of the Spiritual Conquest of Mexico. He was a fanatical defender of the Catholic faith, while the whole of Europe was deep in the upheavals caused by the Reformation and the Counter-Reformation. The first twelve Franciscans arrived in Mexico scarcely four years after the excommunication of Martin Luther; some twenty years later the European bishops were gathering for the Council of Trent (1544–1563). Against this background it is easier to see how a fear of heresy could influence the Friars of America, where they continually were confronted with paganism in its most unpredictable form. Possibly it was this which led to a mistake fatal to the religious future of Mexico: the failure of the Mexican College of Santa Cruz de Tlatelolco. The College was founded to prepare an Indian élite to enter the Christian priesthood and had always been opposed by the other orders in Mexico. The Dominicans, especially, objected that the Indians would never reach the spiritual maturity required of a Catholic preacher. This the Franciscans were unable to refute conclusively, and it must be admitted that they finally lost patience and gave in. However, it is interesting to speculate on the difference that even one single Indian Bishop would have made in those early years.

When, in the 18th century, a lack of priests forced the religious orders to change their minds, it was too late. The new priests, always considered slightly inferior to the Spaniards, became embittered. The start of the veneration of the Virgin under two titles may have been the result of the race-consciousness of the clergy. Our Lady of Guadaloupe became the Patroness of the Indians, and our Lady of the Remedios, the Patroness of the Spaniards.

The wealth of the Church which grew for centuries in a poor country, finished by arousing a sullen resentment. The humility of the first priests with their fine understanding of the Indians gave way to an unbecoming arrogance.

The revolution in the 20th century dispossessed the clergy of all their worldly goods. They lost their convents, monasteries, and churches: and they grew nearer to their parishioners. It would seem that now, with a few rare exceptions, the influence of the church on the Indians is as strong as it was long ago, blending itself with the pre-Columbian traditions and rites, and with the modern concept of the Catholic Church. But, what really does survive is undoubtedly the Face of Christ, which has remained identical and has been worshipped through the years.

43

This woman, not long dead, is propped up on a four poster bed. Some women take their dead babies to images of the Virgin Mary for blessing.

Seri
Mexico

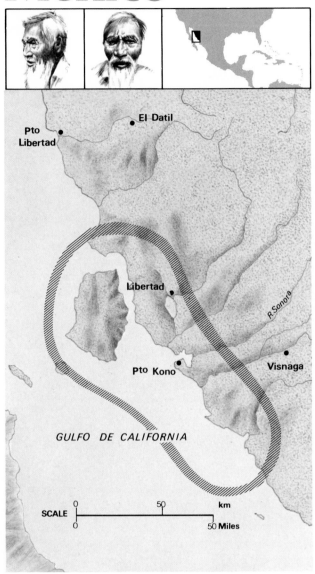

In the north-west corner of Mexico is the state of Sonora. It is bordered in the north by the United States, and in the west by the Sea of Cortés (the Gulf of California). Within this 700 mile long gulf is the largest Mexican island: Tiburon, the traditional home of the Seri Indians. In the early 1960s, the Mexican government forced the Seri to leave their island, and now they live chiefly on the coast of the mainland. There are only about three hundred of these people left, the remnants of several distinct Seri groups. They live in scattered encampments or gathered around the fishing town of Disemboque. But the island of Tiburon is still their true, spiritual home.

They have their own story of creation, like all the peoples of the earth. And the myth of their origins is closely related to their everyday life. For in the beginning

Catching the family dinner
is easy — flick the line in
and flick out a fish. But
the outside world is fast
closing in on Seri life-style.

a huge turtle emerged from the sea and gave the Seri people its home. Indeed the island does look like the back of a turtle, silhouetted against the sky. The turtle gave them a home and he gave them sustenance, and to this day the turtle is the mainstay of their society. They use the huge shell as a shelter, as a cradle for their children, and the flesh as a welcome source of food. And nowadays the turtle brings them pesos. They sell it to the merchants from the nearby city of Hermisillo.

The first report of the Seri Indians came from Cabeza de Vaca, a Spanish explorer, in the 16th century. De Vaca had been shipwrecked off the coast of what is now Texas, and lost his clothes and all he possessed. On his transcontinental journey towards the west coast of Mexico he came to no harm, although he was an alien, a white man, and the tribes he encountered were savage. Dane and Mary Coolidge, in their book published in 1939, describe the Seri of the time as cannibals, 'drinking human blood and eating the flesh raw . . . as proper a race of savages the world has ever seen.' But Cabeza de Vaca showed no fear, winning the tribe's respect by the help he offered them. He amazed them by performing the

Dawn at Disemboque brings
the fishermen home after a
night's fishing. They carry
their catch of tuna ashore
where it will be dried.

first surgical operation they had ever seen. He removed an arrowhead from the chest of one of the Indians, and the man lived. They watched with wonder and were so impressed that they brought him the gift of one thousand deer hearts. They knew about killing, but he knew how to heal, and they were willing to learn from him.

In 1536, de Vaca gave this description of the life of the Seri Indians: 'On the coast there is no maize, the inhabitants eating the powder of rush and of straw, and the fish that is caught from the sea by raft, since they have no canoes.' A scanty report, but enough to show how meagerly the Seri lived. They have *just* survived to this day, with very little change in their way of life.

Their agriculture is still very limited in the coastal desert they inhabit. The Seri live in the most rugged part of Sonora; the land is parched and the least fruitful of the entire province. The sea is still their livelihood, and they still fish from rough rafts, woven from rushes. Since early this century, however, fishing has become a commercial industry. Their catch is now sold to merchants who come in lorries to collect the fish and transport it to the towns. The Indians have wooden dories now, as well as their rafts, and outboard motors instead of the traditional sail. In addition to the age-old hook and line they use explosives to stun or kill the fish. Their most valuable export, the turtle, is often hunted at night, with the help of lanterns and modern harpoon guns.

Like the turtle, the pelican has a sacred meaning in the mythology of the Seri tribe: ancient Seri clans bore the names of Turtle and of Pelican. After this white bird they named the smaller island which lies close beside the isle of the turtle. ('Pelican' means 'white' in Seri language.) Like the turtle, the pelican supplies the Indians with a substantial part of their income. From its skin are made blankets, for export now, or for sale to the visiting tourists.

The Seri were originally more successful than their neighbors in escaping influences from abroad. In the 18th century a Spanish mission was set up among them but they were soon in revolt against it. In 1895 W. J. McGee wrote a report on the tribe and its history, after visiting them briefly. Seri tradition tells of a major battle with the well-armed Spanish troops, and of their gradual retreat towards the sea to take refuge on their sacred island. They were harassed continually by the Spanish and became a race of nomads. Spanish Catholicism has influenced the religions of the Pimo Bajo, the Papago and the Opata – who also inhabit Sonora – but the Seri religion bears no trace of Christianity. Until the 20th century they remained isolated, unaffected and entirely independent.

They were always a proud people: McGee described their appearance in detail. 'They are of splendid physique, fine chests, with slender but sinewy limbs, hair is luxuriant and coarse and is worn long. The Seri are notably vigorous in movement, erect in carriage and remarkable

Seri Indians are now banned
from their traditional home
on Tiburon island across the
sea after being accused of
killing two stranded Mexicans.

The Seri were once described
as 'drinking human blood and
eating the flesh raw . . . as
proper a race of savages as
the world has ever seen.'

For the fishing, the Seri now
use wooden dories instead of
rafts woven from rushes — and
outboard motors instead of
traditional sail and paddle.

47

Seri Mexico

The chief of Disemboque
carves an iron-wood sculpture,
in the shape of a turtle. He
is reputed to be 104 years
old, and is almost blind.

At puberty rites, some Seri
girls paint their faces as
their ancestors did. For
a few days the girl will be
the center of attention.

Outside a shelter a woman
makes a coiled basket with
colored reeds. Women also
make pots with loops of clay
— both are sold to tourists.

for fleetness and endurance.' Coolidge confirms this impression: 'They are a tall and slender people, a nation of runners and so proud were they of their warlike courage that they often left their weapons behind, killing their enemies with their bare hands. They ran down the horses of the settlers on the desert, springing on their withers like mountain lions, and breaking their necks with one twist.'

Present-day visitors to the Seri find them a gentle naïve people, who welcome visitors, particularly those who come from the north and who, traditionally, have brought only kindness. Visitors have brought them gifts as well, and against the background of this primitive people, these 'gifts' often seem intrusive.

Old Ivy League suits, scuffled in the sand, may be among the first things a visitor notices when he arrives at an Indian encampment, or a small Indian girl incongruous in a frilly American party dress: old tires whizzing down the beach, little boys playing baseball. Shelters, which from ancient times have been built of rushes, moss and twigs and the shells of turtles, now incorporate bits of plastic and old sheet metal. It is not the custom of the Indian to pick up anything for which he has no further use: this created no problem when all their waste was organic, and would return to the earth. But plastic bottles, old shoes and tin cans do not. Their litter builds up into mountains and they seem oblivious of the mess. As a matter of fact, litter seems to be a status symbol. Among the more affluent groups the car is a social distinction. The more cars an Indian has, the greater his status; who cares if they are not mobile?

Modern society is beginning to alter their way of life in less tangible ways. Traditionally they have had a system of discipline by which they purge their society of those who offend against it. Any member of the tribe who has committed a crime is banished and must remain an outcast. In an enclosed society, where each man is largely dependent on his neighbor, such ostracism attacks not only the dignity of the offender but also his material well-being. The outlaw might not live long in this desert region without the protection of his tribe. The introduction of commercial trading among the Seri has to some degree broken down this tribal interdependence. Individual gain begins to take precedence over mutual consideration and respect.

The Seri have their ears tuned to the sound of an approaching automobile. The arrival of any visitor is greeted with enthusiasm by the women and children, their arms strung with the necklaces they sell. They show great imagination in the way they put together these treasures from the sea. What at first might appear to be babies in swaddling clothes, which the women stroke constantly, are soon revealed to be pieces of carved ironwood, wrapped for protection in lengths of material or brightly colored shirts. The carving of ironwood is new to them. With the crudest of tools, the machete,

Seri women wear dresses of
brightly colored calico. The
bracelets and necklaces,
made with tiny shells by the
children, are all for sale.

49

A child's face is decorated with painted lines. The colors now come from packet dyes, but once were ground down from rocks and stones.

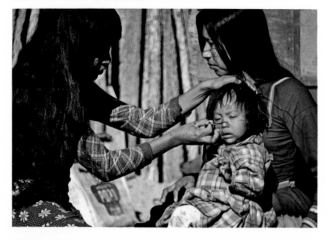

they shape out their basic design. It is always something they know well: a bird or a frog, turtles, fish or human figures. Ironwood is one of the hardest of woods, rich in natural designs of lighter and darker brown. Once the pattern has been blocked out, the figures are polished lovingly by hand.

The hood of one's car is soon covered with these carvings, and the sales-talk of the women is baffling. Some speak Spanish, while the older Indians murmur in their ancient Hokan language. With the money that they make from their carvings and other crafts, the women buy groceries from the village store, run by a Mexican trader. As well as sugar, flour, coffee, watermelon, cucumbers and other foods needed to supplement the Indians' diet of fish and game, the store sells such luxuries as candy, patented medicines, baby powder, and of course the ubiquitous coca-cola.

In the towns and larger villages each family has a hut – *jacal* – of wattle and daub, but in the temporary settlements, set up along the coast by groups of families during the fishing season, their homes are scarcely more than rough windbreaks. These are spread out along the beach, about 60 feet from the sea. The floors of the huts are of mud: there are no tables, beds or chairs. As they have been doing since Cabeza de Vaca first discovered them in 1536, the Seri live on the ground, sleep on the ground and eat on the ground.

The women sit outside the shelters, carving or making the coiled, flat baskets and the pottery which they also coil, scooping out the center of the bowls to give a smooth finish. The children work too, threading strings of tiny shells for necklaces and bracelets.

Each day the Seri men go out to sea, fishing from their dories, and hoping to bring in at least one turtle for the evening meal. If the catch is a good one, the turtles that are not immediately needed for food are kept alive on dry land in a corral. There they may remain for up to a month without food or water, until they are sold to traders or eventually consumed. The turtle is still very often hunted in the traditional way, by means of a wooden harpoon – sometimes as long as 21 feet – with a jagged hook at the end which comes off in the animal's shell. This hook is attached to a rope, secured in the fisherman's boat. Sometimes a turtle may be speared as many as three times. When the turtles are put in the corral the spear holes are cemented to stop bleeding and keep out the flies. Traders pay one peso per kilo for turtles, which normally weigh about 55 kilos.

There is an air of excitement when the boats come in as the women try, from a distance, to see how many turtles are in the catch. They build a fire on the beach, and cook one of the turtles there and then in its shell. McGee reports that the Indians used to eat the turtle flesh raw '. . . if well anhungred, but stopping to singe and smoke or half roast the larger pieces if nearer satiety.'

After their meal some women sew by the light of the

On Puntu Chueca beach a Seri Indian plays his accordion. Silhouetted behind is the island of Tiburon, the Seri's spiritual home.

Puntu Chueca village is cluttered with piles of rubbish beneath a forlorn cross – there is just one Christian missionary.

Once the catch has been landed women dry the fish in the sun, by piercing them through the gills with sticks thrust into the ground.

fire, using torn scraps of material to decorate their ankle-length dresses. They no longer use the skin of the pelican for their clothing, but bright colored calico. They decorate their blouses with multicolored piping, a profusion of buttons, and a distinctive pleated frill at the waist. The men dress in conventional trousers and shirt, sometimes adding the traditional brightly colored kilt on top. A few of the older men still wear their hair long, either loose or in braids.

Some Seri women continue to paint their faces; the main feature of this decoration is a strong, light-colored line which runs across the bridge of the nose and out along the cheek-bones. Beneath this line the patterns are varied and intricate, with tiny dots of color forming triangular or oval designs on the women's cheeks.

This custom most commonly accompanies the rites which are performed for every girl as she reaches puberty. For four days she becomes the center of attraction among her family and is celebrated with chants and singing and the dance of the *pascola*, performed upon a board. During these four days she is believed to be sponsored in her journey into adult life by her elders. The Seri ceremony for the dead – the *amak* – also involves the idea of sponsorship, this time for the journey into the

underworld from which both earth and beings were originally brought by the Pelican and the Turtle.

Marriage plays an important part in the life of the Seri. They are now monogamous, although formerly, when the male population was regularly decimated in battle, it was the custom to take more than one wife. A large bride-price is paid to the parents of the wife, sometimes amounting to hundreds of pesos, and after a period of probation, when the young man must prove his worthiness to the matrons of both families, the young couple go to live in or near the home of the bride's parents. The Seri society depends to a large extent on the rights and obligations of kinship, and is thought to be principally matriarchal, but this is not clear. Their religion too is obscure; it centers generally around the myths and stories of the people's origin.

The fact that little is known of Seri society may help to explain the persistence of their simple way of life. For, since their rejection of Spanish Christianity in the 18th century, they have escaped the attentions and influences of the outside world. But where the Church, the army and the explorer have failed substantially to alter this people, commerce and the tourist may finally succeed.

51

Tarahumara
Mexico

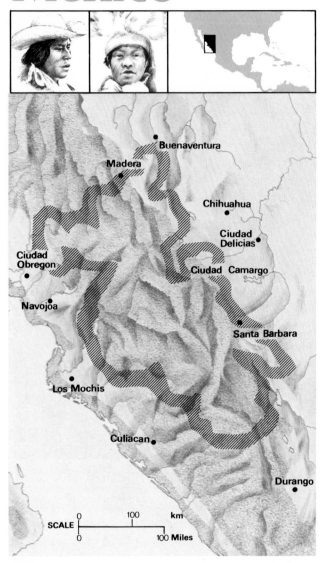

The Tarahumara are one of the few Indian tribes in Mexico to have succeeded in retaining much of their traditional way of life in the face of western civilization, and this in spite of the enormous mineral and timber wealth of their territory. Three factors have particularly helped to preserve their tribal integrity: the inaccessibility of their land, the presence of a Jesuit mission there since 1639 which has acted as a buffer between the Indians and the outside world, and the resilience of their people and culture.

They live in some 26,000 square miles of the Sierra Madre plateau in north-western Mexico, a bare 150 miles from the US border. Most of the land is around 7,000 feet high, is pine-forested and has an alpine climate. Flocks of parrots sweep over the bamboo and orange trees. The southern part of the territory is criss-crossed by a series of volcanic canyons. Some are deeper than the

52

In Chihuahua State, dancers
with painted skin celebrate
Easter. The Judas effigy is
significantly dressed as a
white cowboy.

53

(Left) A Good Friday Christ figure is slung to a pole before burial in the Tarahumara way. 'Policemen' with pikes keep night vigil.

(Below) Drummers make up their faces with chalk and lime. The drums are brought out only for the Easter festivities.

These Easter dancers, who here take a rest on the hillside, use the same type of wooden swords that the Aztecs used against Cortés.

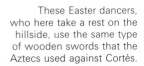

Grand Canyon and plunge almost to sea-level. Here in the south the climate is distinctly tropical, and the wealth of minerals, ranging from gold to copper, is abundantly visible: the walls of the great Copper Canyon literally glitter with color. But this showy *richesse* is a merciless tease: the canyons are so precipitous and inaccessible that none of the great mining companies has yet found it practicable to exploit their wealth.

Occasionally Indians with gold dust wrapped up in a bandana do contact the white people. But they are wary. If an Indian is asked where the dust comes from, his face goes blank and he mumbles 'From the canyons.' He never forgets that Tarahumara who once showed the sources to the white men ended up dead or as slaves in dim tunnels.

In looks and culture the Tarahumara are closer to the North American Indians than to the neighboring Mexican Indians. The men wear loin cloths fashioned out of two pieces of cloth, with a triangle falling over their behinds. Another piece of colorful cloth is folded into a headband – either knotted at the back or, more fashionably modern, attached with a safety pin – so that two long tails fall down their backs. Their sandals are now made of pieces of tires, although they were once of goatskin. The women wear long, brightly-colored skirts and shirts with puffed sleeves. They carry their babies on their backs in a piece of cloth knotted over their breasts. Tarahumara clothes were once made of wool; now they are made of the cheapest, most colorful curtain cloth – one of the few things which they buy from the local Mexican settlers.

Certainly the unique and most fascinating feature of Tarahumara life is the importance they attach to running. They are probably the best long-distance runners in the world, and their inter-village races – together with the Easter and harvest fiestas – are the most important events of the year.

Tarahumara races are up to ten times as long as the 26-mile marathon which is the ultimate test of endurance in the western world. When invited to compete in a

A Tarahumara Easter drummer makes his way alongside a glass-calm river to join fellow celebrants at the Jesuit mission.

55

Hatted long-distance runners
begin the descent into a
canyon. They take turns to
flip the wooden ball
forward with their feet.

famous marathon in Kansas, the Tarahumara sent girls. Tarahumara runners can go non-stop for three days and nights. When the light has gone they carry torches.

Not content simply to run, they are divided into teams, as in *rarijipari* (the men's competition), and either the fastest runner or the best kicker kicks a little wooden ball along the track as they run; the women carry hooked sticks with which they pick up and hurl along a little wooden hoop. The races are run in laps, from two to 20 miles long, along narrow dirt tracks and through thick forest, where the ground may rise and fall by several hundred feet. The inter-village races are occasions for heavy gambling. They bring together people with no settled communities and whose whole way of life tends to be solitary.

Running as a sport has developed from and alongside running as a need. In the hard snow-bound winters Tarahumara hunt deer by running their prey to death. With a dog to keep him on the right trail, a hunter keeps after his prey until after a day or two of continuous chase the deer falls from exhaustion.

The Tarahumara refuse to live in the villages, each with its school and church, set up for them by the Jesuits.

They have never gathered together in either settled or nomadic villages. The shortage of good farm land means that each family often lives a long way from the next. Indeed many Tarahumara 'commute' between three or four widely scattered fields. Most now live in wood shacks, but many – like their fathers – still inhabit caves. During the bitter winters a large number move to the warmth of the canyons.

Their staple diet is maize. They also grow beans and squash – a vegetable of the gourd family like pumpkin. Wheat, introduced by the Jesuits, is becoming more popular. They also pick wild onions and mustard greens.

They hunt small wild animals such as skunks and chipmunks with bow and arrow. They need a strong arm to throw stones into the cliffs' cracks to knock down honeycombs. They fish too – with drugs or 'with thunder.' They dope the water with root juices and the fish float groggily to the surface; or they lob sticks of dynamite into the largest pools and scoop out the fish killed by the blast.

Domestic animals – goats, sheep and cattle – are important to the Tarahumara not because of their meat, but because of their manure which fertilizes the thin soil. They never slaughter domestic animals except as a sacrifice on ceremonial occasions. Nor do they milk the cows except in Mexicanized areas. They keep animals for manure and for other by-products – wool, goatskins, cowhide. Cattle also pull the plows. Dogs herd and guard the sheep, and are never eaten. They like to travel on foot, and so few have horses; *burros* (donkeys), though rare, are the favorite beasts of burden.

In their agriculture, as in nearly everything else, the Tarahumara stick strictly, even defiantly, to the methods of their forefathers. The Jesuits maintain a continuous and concentrated effort to introduce more effective ways of plowing, sowing and harvesting, and they urge the Tarahumara to use fertilizers and pesticides. The

A Tarahumara long-distance
runner carves the wooden
ball that competitors in
the 200-mile race will
kick as they run.

Torch-bearing front-runners
in the three-day non-stop
'marathon' stride out past
bystanding tribesmen in a
flaming streak.

Tarahumara listen with polite indifference, nod their understanding, and continue as before. The fact that they are often desperately short of food and many children die of malnutrition makes not a jot of difference.

Agriculture shapes society. The single family is the basic unit. Children learn to live with solitude early, for they are sent off as soon as they are old enough to look after the flocks and stay away from home up to five days at a time. As a result they are a reserved people, even among themselves, and this is why the occasions when they do congregate tend to be carefully formalized until sufficient quantities of *tesguina* – their corn-alcohol– have lessened their reserve.

Apart from the numerous fiestas and the inter-village races, the Tarahumara get together to help each other; when a man needs to sow or reap, clear land, build a shack or fence a field, he invites all his neighbors to a *tesguinada*. First they work, then they have a feast and get drunk on *tesguina*. This is the sole payment; the host is not obliged to help his neighbors when asked, though it is frowned upon if he does not.

The Tarahumara have had their territory divided into districts, with the Jesuit-built villages as the centers. While they eschew the villages as places of residence they happily use them as social centers, and it is here that each district elects its officials and tries wrongdoers.

Government, kept to a minimum, is by popular consent. The most important officials are the *gobernador* (governor) and his assistants, the *capitanes*. They are usually elected at the Easter fiesta and can be thrown out as easily as they are elected.

Elections are events to be enjoyed. It is considered improper to aspire to office, so the elected official shows intense displeasure at his election – sometimes he even runs away. The whole village then sets off in pursuit. When they catch him they drag the reluctant winner back bodily and present him with his insignia of office: a brazilwood cane with a brass pommel, a spear, a bow and arrow, or – if he is important – a rifle.

The *gobernador* presides at trials and advised by his *capitanes* settles disputes, usually over inheritance. He is also responsible for looking after the village and gives a weekly sermon to the members of the district community; he tells them the laws of the land, castigates or praises them, and orders them to be good. The weekly sermon is the only education many children get.

Trials are solemn affairs and since the Indians tend to be honest, they are rare. The commonest crime is theft. The wrongdoer is brought before the *governador* and his assistants: the rest of the people look on. The accused and witnesses are questioned. Anyone may come forward to speak for the prosecution or defense. The *gobernador* consults his assistants and gives the verdict. Contempt of court is usually punished by doubling the sentence. A public whipping was once the most common punishment, but due to Jesuit pressure a simple talking-to has become more usual. This is just as effective, for the real deterrent for a Tarahumara is humiliation in

57

Tarahumara Mexico

This ill-fed child may yet become a sturdy 'marathon' runner. Foreign experts cannot explain why Tarahumara are such talented athletes.

Mother and child strip maize cobs by a method handed down from Aztecs. They eat meat only on ceremonial occasions.

front of people he has known all his life. For a grave offense a man may be banished from the district; a murderer or unreformed thief is usually handed over to the Mexican authorities in far-off Batopilas.

As well as the *gobernador* and his assistants there are the mayor and his aides, the *fiscales*. One of the mayor's principal functions is that of official match-maker: he goes round consulting parents, introducing young people, settles the financial arrangements, and sets up the affair.

Then there is the shaman, the medicine-man of which there may be several in a district. His knowledge is so secret that he passes it on only to his chosen son if he has one or, if not, to an apprentice. The shaman is a highly respected and slightly feared figure and lives well, since he is asked to solve nearly all problems of health or spirit. The usual payment is a *tesguinada* and some food.

Each shaman has his own methods. Some specialize in herbal medicine, others favor steam-baths and massage. Many now get hold of modern drugs and – as is so common in the west – any old pill is believed to cure almost any illness. Some also use the *peyote* plant, which gives hallucinations. But the Tarahumara use it less than the neighboring tribes. When a man suffers a snakebite, he has smoke blown in his face or he is told to chew *peyote* buttons. If the offending snake is caught, the victim is instructed to bite it back. Only when the shaman has failed hopelessly is a dying man taken to Jesuit doctors.

The shaman is important because he is the core of Tarahumara conservatism. With his secrecy, his knowledge of ceremony and ritual and his attachment to the old religion, he is the guardian of Indian culture and a pillar of strength against the Jesuits and other western influences. And it is not only because of superstition or ritual that the Indians continue to use the shaman; he really is a doctor and he does cure most Tarahumara ills.

Tarahumara religious customs and beliefs have been so infiltrated by Christianity that they are now a fascinating, often bizarre mixture of the pagan and the Christian. The experience and common sense of the Jesuits have certainly saved the Tarahumara from the fate suffered by many other tribes where missionaries have destroyed an active ancient and complex system of belief and practice and replaced it at one clumsy sweep with Christian culture. The result has varied from bloodshed to alcoholism to a simple slow and tragic fading away of Indian dignity and sense of identity. The Tarahumara have kept dignity and pride, a spiritual and material self-sufficiency.

The Tarahumara believes that his soul is his breath. When he dies his breath goes to heaven, while the shell, his body, decays on earth. When his body is cold, his soul is hot; breathing on his hands will warm them. In dreams his soul wanders and must beware of the whirlwind, the whirlpool and the rainbow: there lurk evil spirits who will snatch away the soul and make him ill.

The Tarahumara take advice from both the *shaman* (the medicine-men) and the Catholic priests. Here the family head awaits a Jesuit.

The shaman must then go to ransom the soul from the spirits. Death is the land of opposites – night on earth is day in the land of the dead, and when it is warm down here it is cold 'up there.'

The symbol of the Four Directions is important, as it is with many North American Indians. The cross probably existed before Christianity and helped to make it acceptable. For the Tarahumara, the cross of Christ represents the four gates: east is the gate where Christ was born; north is the gate of the *gobernador* and the officials; south is the seat of the Virgin of Guadeloupe; west is the home of the three animals – the fox, whose bark means the death of a man; the owl, whose hoot warns of a woman's demise; and the oko-bird who with its cawing announces the death of a child.

The future of the Tarahumara is bleak and uncertain. In spite of their present survival and their growth in numbers, the western world is constantly encroaching on both their land and their way of life. The vast pine forests attract the Mexican timber concerns. They pay the Tarahumara, who have virtually no concept of money, a ridiculously low price for areas they desecrate. Settlers get hold of the best Tarahumara land by offering sums of cash which the Indians cannot resist.

But this whole process is softened by the Jesuit presence. The missionaries are constantly guarding the Indians' rights. They are far from being obsessive converters. Their main services to the Tarahumara are medical and educational. Yet the Jesuits too are a threat: Christian culture willy-nilly destroys the Indian one, and the increasing Jesuit concentration on getting the children to school is probably the most subversive influence of all.

The Jesuits provide desperately needed medical aid. Some 75 per cent of Tarahumara children die before they are five years old, mostly of malnutrition or tuberculosis. The Jesuits condemn birth control and the balance of nature might soon be substantially altered by western medicine. If the Tarahumara population explodes, many of them will have to leave the land. The pattern of life will be drastically changed.

While accepting their protection, the Tarahumara have so far evaded the Jesuits' influence fairly successfully. When the first Jesuit mission arrived in 1639 there was bloodshed, but now the Tarahumara resist passively. They simply do not put Jesuit suggestions into practice. They avoid the Jesuit hospital if they possibly can. They may attend a Christian service in the village church, but will follow it with a service of their own. The children who attend the Jesuit boarding-school for one reason or another – usually because they are orphans – are shunned and usually leave the district altogether. The children who go to the village school and listen to classes broadcast by radio from Sisoguichic, forget all they learn as they grow up. Then they happily resume normal Tarahumara life.

Huichol
Mexico

Shaman Ramon Medina leads
a yearly pilgrimage to gather
peyote, a hallucinogenic drug
the Huichol believe enables
them to 'walk with the gods.'

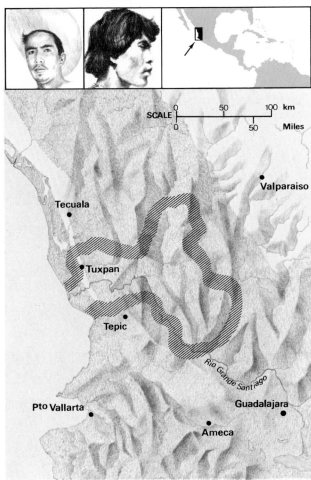

Just as it is the Muslim's lifelong desire to make his pilgrimage to Mecca, it is the supreme ambition of the Huichol Indians one day to take part in the annual expedition which brings to these people their necessary supplies of *peyote*.

Together with the corn and the deer, with which it is mystically associated, the *peyote* plant plays a most important part in the religious and social life of the Huichol. Its name is a Spanish version of the Nahuatl word *peyotl*, a spineless cactus which grows in Central Mexico, in a desert region some four hundred miles to the east of where the Huichol live. It resembles a green carrot, and has an extremely unpleasant taste; but it contains the drug mescalin, which is a powerful hallucinogen, and anybody who has read Aldous Huxley's book *The Doors of Perception* – or knows of the effects of LSD – will understand what the Huichol mean when they claim that *peyote* enables them to 'walk with the gods'.

They live in the Sierra Madre mountains of northern Jalisco and Naharit, not easily accessible, and thus cut off from the rest of the world. They have preserved their 61

Huichol women dress
exuberantly: ear-rings, head
ribbons, necklaces, bracelets
with their vividly embroidered
wool or cotton tunics.

Huichol girls marry as young
as 13. Polygamy is common;
adultery is tolerated; but
seducers of unmarried girls
are punished by flogging.

original speech – a Uto-Aztecan language – in exceptionally pure form. Their social patterns have been modified
by Spanish and Mexican authority and their religion by
Catholicism, but in neither case profoundly. Their
territory extends for about forty miles from north to
south and about twenty-five miles from east to west. It is
a land of high mountains, which rise to eight or nine
thousand feet and are covered with pine-forests. At the
higher altitudes there are many Sonoran deer and pec-
caries which the Huichol hunt at religious feasts. And
down in the valleys, and by the Rio Chapalagne where
the climate is sub-tropical, they fish and tend their
bananas and sugar-cane and cotton. But their homes are
mostly established at medium altitude, where the climate
is kindest.

On the whole the Huichol prefer not to live in villages,
which are chiefly occupied by their officials, who are
elected in a remarkable way. The election of the officials
is in the hands of *curanderos*, who are mystics, sooth-
sayers and medicine-men, and exercise this responsibility
entirely in the state of trance induced by *peyote*.

The people generally live on *rancherias*. Their lives
are agricultural and devoted to raising the corn and beans
and squash that form their chief diet, together with
smaller quantities of amaranth, tomatoes, melons, chili,
and gourds, tobacco, lemons, peaches, and other vegetables and fruits. A *rancheria* has no precise American or
European equivalent: it is a settlement smaller than a
village or *pueblo*, occupied by a group of related families,
united among themselves but with a strong sense of
collective independence. Compared with the society of
the Pueblo Indians (which resembles theirs in many ways)
Huichol society as a whole is loosely structured and
decentralized.

Within each *rancheria* there will be several houses,
circular or rectangular, built round a roughly circular
patio and surrounded by a low rock wall. Clay, poles,
rocks, and adobe are the usual building materials. The
roofs are thatched with palm or grass. Each house has an

adjacent but separate kitchen and granary, in which the
family treasures may be stored as well. The indoor
furnishings are simple, since the Huichol live mostly
out-of-doors: there will be a fireplace, a griddle for
tortillas, a stool or two, perhaps a ceremonial chair or a
bamboo bed, though it is usual to sleep on hides or mats
on the floor.

The Huichol dress colorfully. The women wear wrap-
round skirts almost to the ankles, and shirts, tunics or
blouses once made of wool but now more commonly
made of cotton. Women who can afford it wear several
tunics. All these garments, together with the head-
ribbons and the blanket or shoulder-robe, are richly
embroidered in traditional designs. Necklaces and
bracelets add to the effect. The men dress in similarly
colorful fashion, with white shirts and loose trousers or
short breeches and with one or more belts of brilliantly-
woven wool or cotton. A shawl or cape and a broad hat
complete their costume; in addition, it is usual to carry a
morral or shoulder-bag, also richly embroidered with
abstract patterns or stylized figures of animals, and often

The body of Miguel Garcia, shot and hidden under a hut-roof was discovered as a result of the shaman's extra-sensory perception.

A fig tree: symbol of a soul's 5-day journey to the land of the dead, carrying evidence of its sexual life—females with male organs and vice versa.

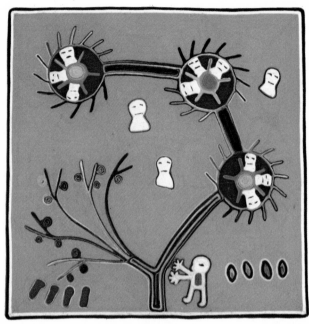

a great many smaller bags as well, which are now primarily ornamental.

This elaborately colorful clothing reflects the temperament of the Huichol, and their traditional way of life which was a fairly easy one. It was not wholly taken up with the problems of survival but allowed scope for relaxation and enjoyment. They are a happy, sociable people, somewhat volatile and prone to anger, but then quick to make peace. They tend to get drunk at festivals, but seldom otherwise. They marry young – the men at fifteen, the women as young as thirteen – in the old days after a brief period of trial marriage. A few Huichol men have more than one wife, and among the others, adultery seems fairly common, and taken lightly.

As in most technically primitive societies, the birthrate is high but so is the rate of infant mortality: most families raise three or four children. There are some 7,000 Huichol now, as against 3,000 early in the century. Huichol children lead happy lives and are seldom punished. Twins, however, are looked upon as bad luck: they are believed to be begotten by a werewolf

disguised as the husband of the unfortunate mother.

The expectation of life is high; many Huichol live to an old age. If they fall ill, there is little attempt at medicine, and no surgery: disease is regarded as a punishment for neglecting some god, and will therefore be treated by prayers and incantations. Death is followed by mourning and by a ceremony that resembles an Irish wake. The dead are apparently not revered or feared in any special way, and are assumed to have passed on to a region in the west.

The Huichol are an intensely religious people. Although their archaic religion is now mildly tinged with Catholicism, it still centers around the importance of producing rain. They have many temples and many gods. The gods are attributed family relationships – 'our uncle', 'our grandfather' – as well as names. Some artifacts – arrows, shields, carved discs, and richly-ornamented bowls made from gourds – are believed to have great supernatural power as intermediaries between gods and men. And behind the very complex religious mythology of the Huichol there lies a simple trinity: the deer, which were their chief food at one time and once the embodiment of their principal god, the corn which has replaced the deer and the rain which enables the corn to grow. These three things are mystically one, as they are with the *peyote* which is also called by the deer's ritual name of *hicuri*, and which brings them a sense of union with their gods.

Peyote has to be collected from a far desert place. And so, each October, a party of eight to twelve men set forth to find it. For some weeks previously, these chosen men have abstained from sex and participated in various religious ceremonies. After a sacrifice, they go forth 63

(Over page) Huichol art is devotional: the shaman is chief artist and works a *nearika* wool painting from a hallucinogenic vision.

Huichol Mexico

These children live in a
mission, but like all
Huichol children their
parents indulge them far more
than western parents would.

from the temple. One man remains behind, to maintain contact between them and the gods: he has already been on the *peyote* pilgrimage, knows the road, follows them in his thoughts and prays constantly. He knows that the journey will take forty-three days; he has a string with forty-three knots in it, and he unties one knot every day. The leader of the pilgrims has a similar string, and thus they keep in touch.

On the fourth day they sit around a fire and confess their adulteries, knotting another string once for each lapse and then throwing that string onto the fire. Absolved and purified they proceed, now fasting almost completely. On the nineteenth day they arrive at the sacred place where the *peyote* was created and is now found. They make respectful sacrifice and pray to be saved from madness, a real danger during the next few days, when they will be gorging themselves on *peyote*, while fasting at the same time. Rather than harvesting the *peyote*, they 'hunt' it like the sacred deer with which it is associated. When they see the cactus, they shoot off two arrows from different angles, to cross behind it and cut off its retreat. Then, very carefully, and praying for forgiveness as they do so, they dig it up.

After four or five days the homeward journey begins; and the pilgrims now fast completely, using only *peyote* to keep them going, and staining their faces with its

yellow juice. They reach home on the 42nd day, utterly exhausted and barely recognizable. At the sacred feast to celebrate their return they are then obliged to get very drunk: the Huichol believe it is dangerous to have anything to do with the gods when completely sober.

They are now stocked up with a year's supply of *peyote*. They keep it by threading the cactuses on strings which they hang on the walls of temples and houses, or sometimes on the ground under a straw covering. Their land is now ritually insured against drought during the following year. The cycle of planting and harvesting can begin.

First there is an extended '*peyote* festival', during which the people eat the newly-collected cactus regularly and so live in a permanent state of exaltation. They are not intoxicated, as with alcohol: in fact their physical balance is better than usual, and they are exceptionally well able to endure hunger, thirst and fatigue. A number of deer must be killed before the festival can begin; they serve as a symbol of nourishment and fertility, and their blood is sprinkled on the grains of corn before sowing. Finally in March or April – some time before the dry season ends – there is a ceremonial baking or parching of corn over the fire, originally to secure the protection of the fire-god, so that the fields could be burnt off for planting without risk of disastrous conflagrations.

In his feathered ceremonial hat, with his sacred arrow and staff in his belt, the Huichol Governor arrives to investigate murder (p 63).

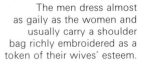
The men dress almost as gaily as the women and usually carry a shoulder bag richly embroidered as a token of their wives' esteem.

In all these rituals, the point is the same: the fiery gods of the dry season must be placated, and the rains brought on, by an invocation of the mystery which is at once the deer, the corn, and the *peyote*. When the rains come, at the beginning of June, there are further, spectacular ceremonies, directed now to the goddesses of rain and water, the natural enemies of the masculine gods of fire and the sun, who must be placated and invoked while the corn is growing. In October, when the green corn ceases to need rain and needs sun instead to harden and ripen it, a further and somewhat ambiguous ceremony then takes place, addressed at once to the wet-season goddesses of rain and water and the dry-season gods of fire and the sun. In some ways it resembles the 'harvest festivals' of Europe. The year's cycle ends with the greatest of all Huichol ceremonies: a fertility-rite of an explicitly sexual character, and the ritual eating of corn-cakes *(tamales)* made from the newly-harvested crop.

The Mexican authorities are well aware of the value and interest of this and other old cultures in their country, and have mounted a fine display of Huichol life and artifacts in the Mexican National Museum of Anthropology: it is possible that they will succeed in their attempts to keep the wise and colorful life-style of the Huichol in being.

The agriculture of Huichol *rancherias* is productive so life is not a struggle and daily tasks can be done in a leisurely way.

Life in a Mexican mestizo village

Our village which has about 800 inhabitants is in the state of Morelos just south of Mexico City. It is a *mestizo* village: the mixed culture and race of the villagers derives from their mixed Indian and Spanish colonial heritage. The village clusters higgledy-piggledy round a little open square, in a fertile valley of the central Mexican plateau.

The dwellings jostle each other and the people live noisily cheek by jowl, but the villagers' lives are entirely devoted to agriculture. They grow rice, corn, beans, tomatoes and – most important – sugar cane.

The climate is almost tropical and never cold. At noon when the sun is baking, the men go to the bar where the stone floor is cool, the flies less bothersome, and the wine good. Some might choose the shade of a fig-tree. Women sit in their doorways gazing peacefully at the little world around them. But at least the village is cooler than on the Mexican coast with its steamy discomfort and stone or concrete pavements that burn bare feet.

Before the Agrarian Revolution of 1910–1917 the village was a *hacienda* – the large private estate given or sold to the Spanish *hacendado* or colonizer by the Spanish Crown. Workers were invited to settle on the estate and given rights to buy goods on credit, to be repaid through their labor. As the simple villagers, or *peóns*, bought more goods on credit than they could ever repay they were virtual prisoners of their *señor*, bound to toil for him forever with little hope of release. The village as it is today is a product of the revolution. Now the land, formerly all property of the *hacendado*, is divided among the villagers by a system of partitioning and tenure known as the *ejido*. But although one of the revolution's principal goals was to end the *hacienda* system and the village was at the heart of the revolution, the old system has left an indelible mark.

In the days of the *hacienda* system the *peóns* would petition their all-powerful *patrón* for his favors. Often the *patrón* was an absentee landowner; then the *peón's* only resort was to appeal to the owner's agent in hope of kindness. When the *hacienda* system ended, half a dozen *patroncitos* replaced the village *patrón*. They were supposed to dole out all the goods that the *patrón* had piled up by his enterprise and by the *peóns'* labor. At best the redistribution of wealth was haphazard. Often the *patroncitos* emulated their former lords' worst traits. Or each would pass the buck of responsibility to his five colleagues. The lot of the villager on the whole deteriorated.

Dulled by the fatalism born of generations of exploitation, the post-revolutionary *peóns* seldom question the right of a political leader or the wealthiest man in the village, who are often one and the same, to behave like a feudal lord. They simply hope that he will be a good feudal lord. A good *patrón* somehow gives back what he has taken from the village. He repairs the school or

Girls play the role of mother
at an early age. While the
real mother breastfeeds baby,
the 8-year-old girl launders
on a stone washboard.

Mexican mestizo village

The *junta*, the team of
yoked oxen, is used by most
villagers for plowing.
Maize, beans and (in the
lowlands) rice are usual crops.

donates a large sum of money for a saint's festival. He is
certainly expected to be generous during the *posadas*,
the night before Christmas when carollers sing for food
and drink. The *hacienda* system is over in name alone.

In a village like ours which is poor and where life is
uneventful, the after-lunch siesta is the treasured part of
the daily routine. After the midday meal everyone –
even bouncy children – settle down to a quiet few hours'
doze. For some the siesta continues throughout the day.
There are many alcoholics and a frequently replenished
pipe of marijuana keeps many a villager hazily content
the whole day long. A lot of them have heard how the
gringos – the people from the USA – have discovered
the pleasures of marijuana, so they sow their fields with
'grass.' (The US government regularly puts pressure on
the Mexican authorities to stamp this out.)

But the villagers who pride themselves on being
advanced disdain marijuana as an Indian invention. The
need to be more Spanish than Indian is universal in
Mexican villages. Some features of traditional Indian life
are hard to throw off. The mothers like to rock babies in
old-fashioned Indian hammocks – but at the same time
they jokingly deprecate them as 'silly Indian things.'
Many children are taught to comb their hair into 'permanent waves' which distinguish them from the lank-

70

Unlike shy Indians, fearful
of the 'magic eye' *mestizo*
villagers confront
the camera with a severe
portrait pose.

This old villager sublets his poor plot so that he can spend his day in a haze of tequila (liquor made from *Agave Tequilana*) and marijuana.

haired pure Indians. If a woman can grow hair on her legs – indicating more Spanish blood than Indian – the hairs are emphasized not shaved. In the more Indian villages the people nervously giggle when photographed, but in villages where the population is more mixed, people pride themselves on their severe and sophisticated portrait pose. *Mestizo* culture is not yet a complete and happy union of Spanish and Indian. The new life has undermined the old but not overwhelmed it: the two strains have not yet made a whole. Both collectively and individually there seems to be a struggle for identity.

All Mexican villagers zealously play the role they think they should adopt. Men and women tend to be type-cast in traditional categories. A man may be a *macho*, the virile daring male; he may be the 'true man', less assertively self-confident than the *macho*; or his fate may be as *el abandonado*, the deserted husband or jilted lover. A woman may be a *macha* and independent and strong-willed, or if she is less overbearing an 'ideal woman'; or alternatively she may find herself *la abandonada*, the deserted wife or mistress. These are the roles. If they are not always precisely fulfilled they certainly color people's hopes and affect their relationships.

A woman is brought up to assume that men are weak, irresponsible, immature and likely to abandon their womenfolk. She expects a man to treat her and their children with capricious violence, to drink hard and regularly threaten her with infidelity. She may hope for better things as she has known better men. But she expects the worst. A girl learns what she can expect from men at her mother's knee. Her mother teaches her not to look forward to a rosy married life, how to defend herself when the worst happens and how to stand on her own feet. She will also instruct her in the important art of feigning submission.

The daughter is never likely to dream of marrying and living happily ever after. When she marries she bases her security not in her potentially faithless husband but on her own daughters and her sons. If her husband does not mistreat or abandon her then she is fully prepared to lose him through violence: he may be one of 30 men killed in the village over the past 30 years, or he may have fled after killing somebody else. This region of Mexico only recently boasted the highest murder-rate in the world. And if loss comes neither through other women nor through violence then there is always the lure of the United States. Many heads of families have made off there as migrant labor. There are many ways in which a woman can become *desamparada* – without a helpmate.

The man too learns his expectation of being *el abandonado* at the knee of his mother. Any woman, he learns, except of course his mother, can be expected to be the 'bad woman' who will cruelly and unjustly set him aside. He loves his mother; possibly he is dominated by her. And she ensures the continuity of marital discord 71

Mexican mestizo village

Bulls are rounded up for the *jaripeo*, the village bullfight where hopeful matadors display a combination of valor and theatrical humility.

Mestizo mothers comb their girls' hair into Spanish-looking 'permanent waves' and jokingly deprecate hammocks as 'silly Indian things.'

The favorite dish is the *tortilla* made from these cobs which mothers energetically grind into *mixtamal* flour.

between one generation and the next. She depends for her only security on her son's mistrust of all other women and his continuing demand for her consolation and affection. So the boy grows into a man as weak and suspicious as the women expect him to be. The mother ensures the continuity of marital discord from her generation to his. The circle of mistrust is complete.

The young man grows up singing songs that celebrate *macho* adventures in which the woman who might hurt him is belittled. The guitarist usually sings a melancholy tune, plucking familiar lugubrious chords. He may not be a budding Segovia, but he convinces himself that justice is on his side.

More often than not the families in our village are fatherless. Each family of mother and children, with or without a father, tries to stand on its own feet. A roof over the family's head, bringing up children, feeding and clothing them are nobody else's business. Help is neither sought nor given. Before the Spanish Conquest the extended family – going back several generations and including cousins, uncles and aunts, who often all lived together – was part of the Indians' clan system. This has now broken down, as happens all over the world when the decline of tribal cultures is accelerated by integration into expanding industrial societies. Increasingly the nuclear family of mother, father and their children stands alone.

In our village several nuclear families will sometimes share the same house site. But if families share a house with relatives they assume this is only temporary. Newly-weds sometimes set up home with the husband's family, but prefer to make their own home elsewhere. A girl is much more likely than a man to marry away from her home village. A husband who comes to live with his wife's family is probably a newcomer to the village.

Marriages between different types – rich and poor, Spanish-looking and Indian-looking, middle-aged men and very young women – are disapproved of. People of 'dubious morality', particularly, should stick to their own kind. Girls are expected to marry in accordance with their mother's wishes. When women in our village marry against their mother's will the community is shocked: children should obey their parents. Boys are expected to go through a difficult rebellious patch, but girls should always be obedient.

Disobedience to your mother is considered a terrible sin. The mother is chief disciplinarian and the discipline tends to be harsh. According to village custom a truly loving parent will frequently mete out corporal punishment. A mother can often be heard to declare that a child should be beaten well and often, especially when it is too young to understand a scolding. The child must be kept in the home, by force if necessary, away from the streets full of temptation, corruption and bad companions.

Husbands and wives often do, in accordance with

Deserted mothers stoically carry on looking after their families, sharpening the taste of the daily fare with chilies and other hot spices.

The *hacienda*, enclosed by the wall, was once a Spanish colonist's estate. Parcelling out the land to peasants has not left them much better off.

The bishop has arrived! *Mestizo* women, faces full of love and devotion, throng to the gates of the churchyard.

expectation, get on badly. Many separate, and wives are rarely surprised when they suddenly have to look after a large family single-handed. In our Mexican village fatherless families are almost as common as families in which the parents have stayed together.

From childhood daughters share their mothers' work – doing the chores, minding the younger children, helping with the cooking. Mother and daughters together often make *tortillas* – a kind of pancake of *mixtamal* flour which they grind themselves from corn. Another regular dish is *frijoles refritos* – beans boiled, then fried in fat. The food would be dull, possibly inedible, were it not strongly spiced with chilies and washed down with wine.

Boys have to reconcile the bravado of being *macho* and virile with the need to be obedient and submissive. So he joins in bullfights in the village; he demonstrates that he is not easily tied down by fiancée or wife and carries on with several other women throughout his marriage. And he threatens violence at the faintest suggestion that his personal honor is tarnished. These days he might strive to be the best basketball player in the village. As boys become youths, discipline weakens. But girls are controlled more strictly than ever. Their morals are jealously watched over.

The eldest son inherits the whole *ejido* – the family plot. The sons who are left out stoically accept the situation. They recognize that family resources are scant and that the eldest son has the rights. They just have to seek other ways of looking after themselves. And landless sons are often content when they see that many farmers are poorer than men who follow even humble trades. In several families the older son has gained another trade – perhaps he is a mechanic – and gladly passes on his inheritance to a younger brother. In some families a son inherits because he is the least educated. Few men seem to resent inheriting no land at all. Everyone, landless and landowner alike, jests of the day when he will leave the village and go off to Mexico City to become a famous bullfighter.

The *jaripeo* – the village bullfight – is a great occasion. The day before, men on horseback round up the bulls. Youths put up sturdy barricades to form the arena. The bulls may not be the power-packed monsters of Madrid or Mexico City, but even a scrawny one stands a chance of knocking down the village's unsophisticated matadors.

The villagers all put on their Sunday best. Boys dangling smartly-booted legs – they are wearing *huaranches*, real shoes – perch cockily on the barricades, showing off their bravery so close to the bull. Everyone wears his broadest-brimmed sombrero. Only the haughty affect disdain for such foolery. They play cards in a nearby café. But if there is human bloodshed – at which no villager conceals his glee – even the card-players throw in their hands and rush to the ringside to glimpse the gore.

The matador himself has a golden opportunity to

flaunt his combined virtues of flashy bravery and elegantly simulated humility which in the eye of a Mexican villager make a 'man of honor.' If the crowd gives him a warm reception, he might be inspired to journey to Mexico City, when celebrated Spanish matadors come across in winter to display their magic.

The village hopeful queues all night for a ringside seat. Watching the grace and dignity of the Spanish heroes, he wishes he too were able to mesmerize the vast bull and huge hushed crowd alike. He picks his moment. Armed with a newspaper, he vaults the barricade, runs up to the bull and performs a few *veronicas*, coaxing the bull into slow tortuous circles, its vicious horns lunging at the taunting newspaper. Officials solemnly escort the villager away, but if the famous matador or the city crowd enjoyed the brief show, he may have achieved his crucial 'break.' He may stay in the city and become apprenticed to a top matador. And who knows? He himself may one day be famous.

The brassy gaiety of the village band led by the local *cacique* (political leader) celebrates the opening of the village bullfight.

For generations *mestizo* villagers have been used to being in debt but card games, for stakes they can ill afford, are popular.

Tarascan
Mexico

Tarascan Indian fishermen
surround their quarry on Lake
Patzcuaro, 7,000 feet up in
the mountainous empire of
the ancient Tarascan.

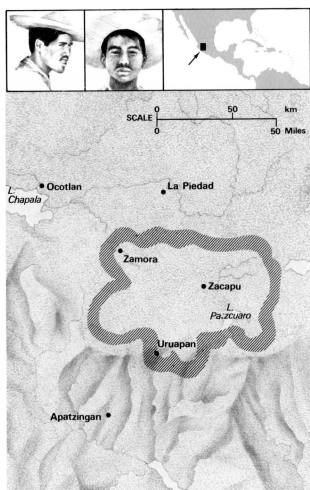

The Tarascan first founded their empire in the 14th century on the shores of Lake Patzcuaro. It was a civilization which, until the arrival of Cortés 200 years later, was to rival that of the Aztecs. Their golden empire and pagan gods once ruled supreme throughout the mountains; craftsmen turned out copper tools, mosaics of brilliant feathers, idols carved from stone and dazzling lacquer works. In times of war, high priests in richly feathered capes called the young men to arms and painted warriors and officers in jeweled clothes gathered behind the banners. Their great cities were built with stone monuments which testified to the glory of their empire.

The Tarascan civilization was to end in a matter of weeks, conquered first by the Spanish soldiery and then by other Spaniards who came in their wake, avid for gold. The Spaniards took over the Tarascan territory and starved and enslaved the people. But the Tarascan were not crushed.

For the 90,000 Tarascan Indians who live today in south-west Mexico, the green mountains of Michoacan

Tarascan Mexico

After their long morning in their canoes, Tarascan fishermen have earned an afternoon of shade and ease in their lakeshore village.

In the afternoon *mariposa* nets are hung out to dry. The Tarascan Indians from the sierra come to the lake to trade their products for fish.

The graceful, winglike *mariposa* nets are named after butterflies. Fishermen stir the water with paddles, then skilfully dip their nets.

While his sons man the canoes,
papacito spends his day
making or mending the nets,
or weaving baskets and
mats from reeds.

Tarascan Mexico

Tarascan women spin wool for cloth to make shoulder blankets, shawls and sashes and to embroider their blouses in brilliant colors.

It is the women who travel throughout the sierra and lakeside villages to sell flowers, pottery, blankets, baskets and *copal* incense.

have been a refuge since the decline of their brilliant empire. The mountains, covered by thick conifer forests, rise to peaks of more than 10,000 feet and for some three months of the year are blighted by frost. The sierra seems out of place in Mexico, which is elsewhere so hot and arid. There are also wide fertile plains and valleys, places where the Tarascan settlements prospered. In their villages high up in the mountains, on the plains and around Lake Patzcuaro the Tarascan have been removed from the events which have had great influence on the rest of Mexico.

Ten years after the Spanish Conquest, the Franciscan missionary Don Vasco de Quiroga followed the Tarascan into the mountains. He brought them new hope: with his help and guidance, new towns and villages were built and the Tarascan arts and crafts revived. He brought them Christianity. Though the empire could not be resurrected, Tarascan culture in part recovered its confidence. In the sierra the Tarascan also found immunity from the gradual encroachment of *mestizos* (Spanish-Indians) and their culture which spread through most of Mexico during the next 400 years or so. In their

Some Tarascan families can afford cattle, sheep and pigs — but other families have only a single cow and nothing else but chickens.

mountain refuge the Tarascan resisted these influences; and preserved much of their old life-style. Their skills became as famed as they had been in pre-Cortesian times. Their language survived, unrelated to any other Indian tongue. Today in many of the villages, Tarascan live alongside *mestizos*; but their ways are different and Tarascan are taught in their own language in the schools. In a Spanish-speaking sea, Tarascan is an island.

Throughout the Tarascan sierra the villages are scattered beside cultivated lands that vary from tiny forest clearings to vast flat plains or rolling fields. Many villages owned their lands communally, until in the late 19th and early 20th century ownership fell increasingly into the hands of the rich and powerful. *Mestizo* landlords seized disputed lands. Or they merely moved in and dispossessed Tarascan families. Only with the Mexican revolution (1910–1920) did agrarian reform return land to the Indians. Today almost half all villages have a communal *ejido*, where every family works a plot of about six or seven acres but where harvesting, planting and much of the administration is done communally. In all villages there is also land owned by private individuals, and forested areas, held in common and administered by the village officials.

For most of the Indian farmers, maize is the staple crop, harvested in August, just as the rains come to an end. Tender young maize is eaten with great relish, roasted on the cob or boiled in thick gruels. But the bulk of the crop is allowed to mature until December or January. The harvest is a group activity, kinsmen or members of the same *ejido* working together; in the evenings they finish off the day with story-telling and drinking.

Tarascan consume a liter of maize each day in the form of innumerable *tortillas*. For these, the farmers' wives must for ever grind the maize, pat it out and roast the *tortillas*. Their other main foods are the chili, beans and squash which they grow, and fish from Lake Patzcuaro. The Tarascan fishermen use wooden dug-out canoes, 10 feet wide *mariposa* (butterfly) nets or much larger gill nets, strung together and about 250 yards long. Several families co-operatively work the gill nets and also seine nets, which are only 100 yards long, and sell their catch at the market. *Pescado blanco* (white fish) is a delicacy much sought after by visitors and Tarascan alike. The lake also provides many different kinds of reeds which the Tarascan use to weave mats, on which most of them sleep, and baskets. Their mats and baskets are sold throughout Mexico. They are old skills passed down through generations of Tarascan. On the islands of the lake, fishing and weaving are the only occupations.

Rainfall in the Tarascan sierra is little more than 30 inches a year; during the dry season most villages suffer extreme shortages of water. Then the task of carrying water in large water jugs from streams or wells up to five miles away, falls to the women. Most sierra villages own a forested hill and the Tarascan are skilled lumberjacks who can square off rough logs with extraordinary precision, using only heavy, archaic axes. Mostly they produce heavy beams and shingles – both of which are used in the snug wooden houses with their wide roofs, that typify mountain villages. The men can now earn up to 50 pesos a day (the wage for farming labor is only about 15 pesos a day) working as lumberjacks or furniture makers. With good profits to be made, many forests have been razed; and mountain slopes turn into soil-eroded wastelands where nothing can grow.

Some Tarascan families can afford a number of domestic animals – a few cows, a flock of sheep, chickens and pigs. But other families have only chickens or a single pig. Since much of the farming is co-operative, a village will also have teams of horses or oxen for the plowing. There are other villages wealthy enough to keep more than 3,000 head of cattle or horses; but few are used as food. A fiesta will often specify how many cattle, turkeys or other beasts must be sacrificed, but it is a special occasion. Meat from domestic animals does not make up a significant part of the Tarascan's diet. Until recently wild game provided much of the meat. Deer and rabbits, and ducks from the lake were hunted all the time. Coyotes, a constant threat to other livestock, were also killed. But now the wildlife has been so seriously depleted that a full-time hunter is rare.

Tarascan crafts that were once famous in the pre-Cortesian days have been restored to their ancient eminence throughout Mexico. Guitars, made in the Tarascan village of Paracho, are sought after in Mexico City, the United States and even in Europe. The attitude of many master craftsmen towards their instruments is much like that of a creative artist. The guitars they make are things they hold in affection. In Cocucho they make clay whistles, 'devils' and other figurines; in Tarecuato, embroidered blouses and red and black woollen belts. Elsewhere villages produce blankets, shawls, hats or simply the straw braiding for hats. Each village has its craftsmen, and its speciality.

Women vendors travel throughout the sierra with their small donkeys loaded with the many-colored merchandise, often selling baskets and mats as well. Big fiestas may have as many as a hundred stalls selling craftwork and pottery. Every town and village has at least two fiestas a year (some have many more) in which its patron saint is honored with extravagant celebrations, involving every person in the community and in which every craft and art is represented. At these fiestas the Tarascan honor the Christian God, while at the same time appeasing ancient pagan gods by ritual sacrifices of wealth – in the form of animals, *tortillas* and liquor consumed in one glorious religious beano. Possibly the fiestas are modern versions of the pre-Christian human sacrificial ceremonies. They certainly cost many thousands of pesos, money that poor villages can ill afford. **81**

The canoes on Lake
Patzcuaro are dug out from
single pines felled in
forested sierra, and dragged
down to the lake by oxen.

Fishermen and weavers cross
from Janitzio to the
mainland markets to trade
their fish and baskets
for wood and maize.

Fiestas combine the acquired rituals of Spanish Catholicism with the ancient rituals of Mexican Indians. They are at one social and spiritual occasions – 'they all give him (the Mexican) a chance to reveal himself and to converse with God, country, friends or relations' – although the participation of the priests varies from community to community. In some villages the priests will be involved in all the village's activities, not least the fiesta. In others a priest will confine himself to monthly visits to perform sacraments and give mass. The town of Azajo built a large church, but kept the priests from participating in the organization of its building because 'then we'd never finish.' And then not all towns and villages have a priest in residence and much of the arrangement and planning of fiestas and rituals is left to the local officers of the village. In some places the fiesta has become an exaggerated, almost commercial, affair. In Huansito, for instance, potters from all the surrounding ceramics villages bring their wares to a gathering that attracts 10,000 Indians and *mestizos*.

Bands provide music in all fiestas and each village or town will have at least one resident group of musicians, from a simple ensemble of pipes and drums, to brass bands with ten or twenty pieces. The Tarascan love their music; outsiders admire it, and their musicians contribute an important part in the famous Balet Folklorico de Mexico. But to them, music is simply another kind of work; a means of buying medicines, fruit, firearms and liquor. A good musician may earn 50 pesos a day during a major fiesta and will play at the *mestizo* festivals in the provincial towns.

But not all Tarascan are keen to be so closely involved with the *mestizos*. By their clothes, for example, they maintain a distinction from the *mestizos*. In the poorer villages the men and the women will wear traditional clothes like the sombrero and shoulder blanket to which the women add a shawl, embroidered blouse and dark blue or black skirt with wool sashes and cotton apron. Children are delivered in the Indian fashion with the mother attended only by a number of female relatives. A week later, at the baptism, a man and a woman are appointed not only as the child's godparents – but, also as the co-parents of the child, the *compadres* of the real parents. A relationship marked by respect, loyalty and

On the lake island of
Janitzio, old men perform
dances that lampoon
the arrival of the
Spanish *conquistadores*.

financial obligations is forged between the two sets of parents.

Marriage for young Tarascan is usually preceded by involved negotiations and weeks, or even years, of courtship. It is a time marked by meetings at the well where the girls draw water, speeches to avow undying affection and even some erotic symbolism. In some villages the courtship is followed by a romantic elopement – or even a bride-capture at the well, carried out with the bride's acquiescence – to the home of the boy or one of his uncles. Tarascan marriage disregards economic differences and is a great leveller. There are three marriage ceremonies: a civil ceremony in one of the towns is followed by a Catholic ritual in a church, and then a traditional Tarascan ceremony, which is a celebration and perhaps the one most enjoyed by all. There are dances, feasting and drinking and in the dancing there is much symbolism which recalls the Tarascan's pre-Catholic pagan past.

At first the young couple live with the boy's parents or if this is not possible at the girl's parents' home in an extra room or lean-to adjacent to the parents' house. It is several years before they are able to set up their own house. The Tarascan family normally lives in a house in which rooms are linked by a roofed entry way. Wealthy families have as many as eight rooms, but poorer people may have only one. A blank wall faces the street and an inside yard contains flowers, vegetable gardens and, at the rear, a place for domestic animals. A grandparent, important in the children's education, often lives with the family. Often several families will share a courtyard, perhaps because the men are craftsmen who work together, or perhaps only for the convenience of sharing the wood gathering and farming between two or more men and sharing the care of children and cooking between two or more women. These co-operative groups tend to be flexible; the men often swop jobs and responsibilities. Also the roles of men and women are less rigidly divided than in the *mestizo macho* culture. The only hard and fast restrictions between what men and women may do are that a man will never make *tortillas*, and a woman will not cut timber.

The Tarascan describe their towns and villages as being either 'divided' or 'united'. In many villages there are factions locked in vendetta. In others a strong *cacique* holds sway. Most communities suffer from internal disputes about land, and are only united by conflict with a neighboring village over other lands. They tend to be particularly hostile to the claims on *mestizo* villages. Sometimes there are prolonged litigations in court. More often sniping, ambushes and fire-fights are the weapons employed.

Every village elects three officers for a one-year term: a mayor, a judge and a secretary-treasurer. These three officials administer the village's lands, its irrigation, care of the *plaza*, civic fiestas and the judging of

minor disputes. They also organize the collection of taxes, forest control and the night watch. The mayor represents his village in all its relations with the state, particularly in questions of taxation, elections and serious offences against the law – murderers, however, usually skip town for a while and are rarely bothered after their return. Whenever an important issue arises there is a town meeting conducted with a solemn observance of rules and procedure.

But beneath all this, affecting political relations just as it affects illness, is the Tarascan's belief in magic. Superstition and witchcraft are as real to the Tarascan as a westerner's belief in democracy. The supernatural and the gods are always present: mediums, who are often women, divine their elusive will. The services of a medium are expensive. They may cost as much as 5,000 pesos. But to the Tarascan it is money well spent if they feel that an illness is cured or a political dispute resolved. Despite their Catholicism, the Tarascan still fear their ancient gods. This is an ambivalence that is not easily obliterated; it is deeply ingrained by more than 600 years of Tarascan history.

Lacandon
Mexico

The Lacandon, whose
ancestors were serfs when
their Mayan masters built
Bonampak (c. AD 700), still
inhabit the Chiapas forests.

For four hundred years Mexico has been an ethnic and cultural melting-pot, within which the Spanish and the indigenous elements have been progressively fused and blended, generating a distinctive Mexican unity. Pure-blooded 'Indians' still remain in quantity, directly descended from the Aztecs and the Maya, and the other pre-Columbian peoples of the country. But almost without exception, they have been culturally 'westernized' – or 'Europeanized' – since the Spanish conquerors came to Mexico from the east.

The Lacandon Indians of the extreme south-east are the only notable group who have so far resisted this process of Europeanization. They may not resist it for much longer. Other 'Indian' groups are moving into their territory; modern means of transport are opening up their secret and hitherto inaccessible valleys; missionaries are at work; and a newly revived demand for mahogany is bringing logging-camps and sawmills to a part of the country which has seen very little of industry in the past.

The Lacandon are a small, scattered people, no more than two hundred in number, who live in widely-

86

Few – if any – other groups
have preserved intact their
ancient culture as well as
the Lacandon – of whom 200
survive, deep in the forest.

dispersed family groups in a mountainous and thickly-forested part of Mexico, close to the Guatemalan frontier. Their territory of 39,000 square miles is enclosed by three rivers, the Lacantun, the Usumacinta, and the Jatate. In this vast area, Lacandon society is extremely decentralized. Each village is at least several days' journey from the next, and each one is hidden away in a clearing, perhaps only approachable by water, or by tracks and paths visible only to the Lacandon themselves.

Living in this way and in this kind of country, the Lacandon have always found it easy to minimize their contacts with the outside world. Cortés passed through their country in 1525; and twelve years later, Spanish missionaries tried to convert them and gather them together into towns, but without success. In 1555 two missionaries were killed as were a number of Indians who had accepted baptism; four years later, an expedition against them met with some success but it was not followed up. In 1695, another effort was made to conquer the tribe and bring them together into a specially-established town, but they slipped away and resumed their own lives.

Their full story is not known. But it seems likely that at some point during what we call the Middle Ages, Maya society was disrupted by invaders from outside who took over such cities as Palenque and Yaxchilan. The upper classes of those cities, the rulers and priests and astronomers, apparently emigrated north towards Yucatan; the lower classes just melted away into the nearby forests and it is essentially from them – with some admixture of other stocks – that the Lacandon of today are descended. Their own language records the fact: they call themselves *massewal*, which comes from a Nahuatl word for working or lower-class people. In origin, they are leaderless and impoverished refugees from one of the world's greatest civilizations.

The Lacandon have no kind of central government, no kingship or priesthood in common: within each *caribal* there is a leader or chief of some kind, but the basis of his leadership is varied and uncertain, and he makes little attempt to hold his people together. It is no rare thing for a Lacandon man to leave his community with his wife (or wives) and their children and found a new settlement of his own, clearing the forest and building huts and living there in a new and further degree of isolation and self-sufficiency.

The Lacandon are still a distinctive people, confident and proud. They are short and golden-skinned, and most of them wear their hair long; they no longer artificially deform their skulls, in the ancient fashion of the

A long-haired Lacandon youth holds a prized quetzal bird (the national emblem of Guatemala). Its feathers are used in making headdresses.

A dugout canoe on the river is the quickest form of travel in the forest but the Lacandon are swift on foot too. Both sexes wear long hair and tunics.

Lacandon Mexico

Hammocks are the main item
of furniture in Lacandon huts.
Once they were made from
bark cloth, but nowadays
canvas is bought from outside

PTC — a bitter tasting
chemical — tests Lacandon
heredity: different racial
groups have varying taste
perception.

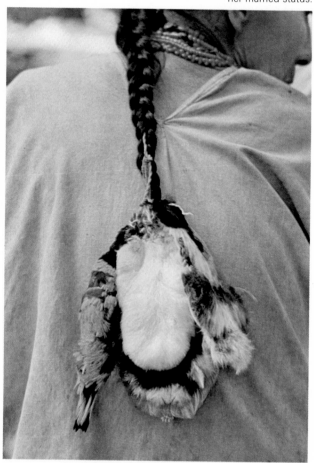

The brightly colored feathers of canaries and other small birds tied to a woman's hair indicate her married status.

country, but they regularly support their burdens by ropes or straps around their foreheads, which consequently are often slightly flattened. They wear no hats, and their clothing is remarkable for its total lack of European influence: over a loin-cloth, they wear a white cotton tunic or poncho reaching below the knees. Some women supplement this with a skirt of the same material, which is sometimes dyed or decorated. The women adorn themselves with a proliferation of necklaces made from beads or berries; the men sometimes wear nose-ornaments.

Elusive and shy, the Lacandon are none the less a hospitable people. A number of European visitors have reported the courtesy and consideration with which guests are received, and the rituals of greeting and farewell which the Indians enact most punctiliously. Their family life appears to be happy; family attachments are strongly felt and little discord arises from their custom of polygamy. Prostitution or adultery are rare, old age is respected, and the looser morality of other societies is regarded with contempt. Drunkenness does occur, but only in connection with religious rites: the gods are believed to look with favor upon a little intoxication, and upon dancing and singing too, but to disapprove of contentions and disputes. Traditionally, the Lacandon govern their behavior accordingly. In many respects they are a most enviably 'civilized' people and admirable in their adherence to their code of morality. They are for example a great deal more honest and generally better-behaved than their neighbors, the Maya of Yucatan.

They are also backward, and rather slow witted. They are not literate and their arts are rudimentary; their technical skills are limited to spinning, weaving, pottery and basket-work; their implements – apart from the machete – are of stone and wood. Their lives are arduous and they work hard. Cleanliness and order are not among their virtues.

Each *caribal* or village is surrounded by jungle, with crops planted in small clearings between felled trees. The houses are little more than shelters. Four forked posts support the framework of a gabled roof, which reaches almost to the ground at each side but is open at both ends: it is covered with palm leaves, which are tied to the framework with flexible vines. A village consists normally of the houses of three or four related families and a temple, resembling a house but rather more carefully built and maintained. At intervals the whole village moves to a new site – usually nearby – in search of fresh land for cultivation.

As elsewhere in Mexico, maize, normally eaten in the form of large *tortillas*, is the chief crop of the Lacandon people and the major part of their diet. They also eat cassava, sweet potatoes, pimentos, beans, chayotes (custard marrows), tomatoes, turtles and their eggs and the plentiful fish and shellfish of the many rivers and lakes of the region. They use nets and rods and lines, and

have developed great skill in shooting fish with wooden-pointed arrows from their dug-out mahogany canoes. For meat they hunt tapirs, wild pigs, wild birds and monkeys. Some keep chickens, which – like bananas – are not native to the country but were introduced by Europeans.

Their social organization was once complex. With the decline in their numbers, it has largely collapsed. Originally they were divided into at least ten clans, each named after an animal. Every man was obliged to marry outside his own clan. The clan names remain, but are no longer taken seriously; and the rule of exogamy, like various other social and matrimonial rules, has broken down under the stress created by a declining population. Polygamy, which is becoming less widespread in this small, scattered community, now occurs almost solely in the families of village chiefs. Young men are sometimes driven to kidnap their brides from other clans, causing inter-tribal vendettas. Such feuds are new to the Lacandon. As late as the beginning of this century, a writer observed that ' . . . they have no wars, nor any occasion for them.'

The Lacandon women cannot be said to have the beauty for which the Maya women of Yucatan are

Lacandon faces have prominent
noses and receding chins but
not receding foreheads, as in
the relief sculpture opposite,
for heads are no longer bound.

This detail on a frieze at
Bonampak dates from the
classical Maya period which
flourished between the 3rd
and 9th centuries AD.

celebrated. They are nearly as strong as the men, and do their full share of the work, cutting the firewood and helping to clear the forest for sowing. Traces still remain of old and widespread fears of the dangerous influences of the female. Women are excluded from most religious rites. Lacandon men make their bows and flint-headed arrows with utmost care, displaying not only an unusually refined technique but also their nearest approach to a high aesthetic sense. It is believed that if bows or arrows have at any stage been in contact with a woman they will never be effective.

The soil of this rain-sodden forest is rich and heavily overgrown. It needs to be cleared, and in the spring, during the relatively dry season, the Lacandon peasant sets to work. First he cuts away the brush and undergrowth from the area he requires, and waits for it to dry out in the heat of the sun; then he piles enough of it around the roots of the trees to set them on fire and bring them down.

Clearing the forest is a special and sacred business, closely related to the problem of survival: the flame used to start these fires must be generated by a method many thousands of years old. At home and for daily use, the Lacandon keep a fire burning continually, never allowing it to go out; on their travels, they use flint and steel and a cotton wick. When burning off the trees the Lacandon Indian takes a piece of soft wood with a hole in it, places a stick of harder wood in the hole, and spins this between his hands. A fine wood-dust is generated and starts to smoulder from the friction. From this he ignites a piece of cotton fluff. As he blows on the flame to get some dry twigs burning, the Lacandon prays to the god of fire. This is the ritual method that the ancient Aztecs used when they kindled the new fire at the top of Uixachtecatl Mountain to begin their sacred cycle of fifty-two years.

The Lacandon are strict in their religious observance. Each village has as its finest building a temple and they put great trouble and time into making incense-burning bowls and images of their gods, and gathering copal gum to make the incense. They also make an annual pilgrimage to the old city of Yaxchilan on the Usumacinta. This city flourished in the 7th century, at the height of the Maya civilization. To this day its statues and reliefs are impressive and suggest holiness and awe. To the Lacandon, who come yearly to burn incense and chant prayers, it is the place of the gods.

Like many Mexicans, the Lacandon have a strong sense of the uncertainty of mortal life. They believe that our present epoch will, like preceding epochs, end in disaster. Some believe that this end will come when a certain headless statue at Yaxchilán regains its head; then jaguars will come in their thousands and devour the human race. Meanwhile their chief anxiety is to placate the rain-god Metsaboc. They live in an exceptionally rainy area; even the dry season – February to April – is showery. Torrential rain is a greater threat to their crops than drought. The sun is a predominantly friendly god. But he has an underground counterpart, Kisin, who causes earthquakes and sickness and through whose territory, with its rivers of ice and fire the sun must pass each night. In this subterranean world the sun, in the character of a mythological hero, contends successfully with the evil Kisin. The Lacandon believe that when a man dies his 'pulse' goes below to live with Kisin in the underworld, while his 'heart' ascends to the high god.

Lacandon religion is permeated by a consciousness of doom; and it suitably corresponds with the actual doom that may now be upon them. Refugees from one high civilization, surviving for centuries in their forest isolation, they are now likely to disappear before the all-smothering tide of another, consumed not by jaguars but by roads and factories.

Perhaps we should go and see whether that statue at Yaxchilan has miraculously regained its head.

Mushroom-ended arrowheads stun birds, knocking them out of trees, but do not damage their highly valued feathers as a pointed arrow would.

Prayer pots are made each year and used for burning incense. The design on this is very similar to one on an ancient Maya pot.

(Center) A missionary lives 200 yards from this farmer but has never converted him: he practises an ancient religion based on natural forces.

Young Lacandon will see changes. This model of a light airplane that landed in a clearing bears no relation to their traditional world.

93

Chamulans of Chiapas

Ancient Maya belief combines
with Catholicism to give the
Chamulans their religion.
Robed officials here
march before the church.

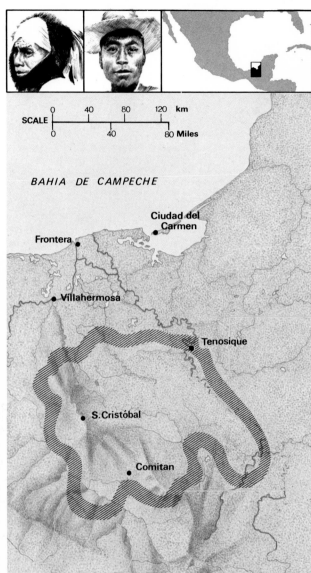

BAHIA DE CAMPECHE

Ciudad del Carmen

Frontera

Villahermosa

Tenosique

S.Cristóbal

Comitan

n the highlands of Mexico's southernmost state of Chiapas they say it took St John the Baptist, Chamula's patron, many years to discover the most desirable homeland in the world. He wandered from place to place until he found hills where he could safely graze his sheep, a people of smooth, clear complexion, and a place where he could build his church. Eventually he built it in the highland region of Chamula. Whenever San Juan (St John) sees that his people are sad, poor, hungry or long to learn a skill or find a spouse, he listens to them on the sole condition that they offer him incense and candles. San Juan has a soft spot for his Chamulan wards and they celebrate fiestas in his honor and play harps and guitars and sing and dance in his praise.

Chamula is one of over 100 Indian communities or

(Below) The music of the harp is sacred to the Chamulans. The harps are taken out of the church only on festival days.

The air is heavy with holy *copal* incense which Chamulans burn as they celebrate the Easter festival.

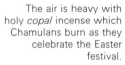

municipios in the state of Chiapas where they speak *Tzotzil*, a Mayan language. The Chamulans' beliefs and rituals too, though modified by Catholicism, are much the same as those of their Maya ancestors. Catholicism has been so reconciled with ancient belief that their religion remains almost as strongly Maya in character as in 1522 when Cortés began the Spanish Conquest. And though *Tzotzil*-speaking Chamula is close to the Mexican town of San Cristóbal de las Casas, and has had its share of missionary attention, it is still one of the most vitally Indian places in the Chiapan highlands. Indeed so distinctively Indian are the Chamulans that Mexican *meztizos* call any Indian, whatever his muncipio, Chamulita, or 'little Chamulan.'

Chamula country is mountainous: pine and oak forests spread across craggy, sharp peaks. Up there the climate is temperate. Under spectacular limestone cliffs you find cool springs and eerie caves. On the rocky and eroded clay soil the Indians grow corn, beans and squash, and raise some livestock. Their houses stand peaceful and stolid, usually without windows, on plots cut into the hillside. Some of the houses are of brick and tile, but the more traditional ones are of wattle and daub, with steeply thatched grass roofs formed into a comb-like stone structure at the top of some Maya temples.

At first the dimness when you go inside makes it hard to see all the bundles and boxes hung around the eaves, the clay pots and gourds on the floor, the ears of corn tied in pairs and slung over the rafters, the plank beds, the men's tiny chairs only two feet high, and the house altar that serves St John and the Maya earth lords alike and often faces the rising sun. The hearth is the heart of the home: men sit on its north side, women on the south. Well before sunrise two noises are already resounding in the house: the swish as women grind corn in metal handmills, and the slap-slap as they shape the tortillas. The men eat first: beans or cabbage, sometimes with potatoes, eggs, dried fish, fruit, onions and occasionally beef or pork. Chamulans have no food taboos, but they do not eat their sheep because they hate the smell of mutton.

Although the density of population on the rocky, eroded mountainside has forced some changes on the Chamulans; and although Spanish Conquest brought Catholic 'conversion' and forcibly extracted labor, goods and taxes from the highland Indians, life in Chamula persists pretty much as it has done for centuries, changing principally in the ways that the Chamulans choose. The Chamulans are proud of *lumal*, their homeland and seldom leave it for good, though many are rich and well-

(Left) Chamulans feast in honor of St John the Baptist, whom they believe to have adopted Chamula because he found it so beautiful.

Even at the laundry,
Chamulans must remember the
earth lords' kindness, or
pukuh witches will assail
them with misfortune.

traveled. And they are proud of their history of up-risings, often in quest of more land: in 1870 they threatened the very gates of San Cristóbal. Until the mid 1930s no Indian was allowed to walk on the sidewalks of San Cristóbal, and they were consistently cheated in stores. Their status has improved, but they are treated as far from equal by the *meztizo* (or *ladino*) population.

While the Chamulans look to the church and the government in Chamula Center – the chief town of the region – for spiritual and political guidance, they draw sustenance from the traditions of their ancestors. A well organized Mexican civil government maintains order, but to Chamulans the true owners of the land are the earth lords, whose sacred homes are in the mountains and caves. Although the saints in their church look like many of the wood and plaster images which grace Catholic churches, to the Chamulans they are primarily Maya earth lords who have chosen Chamula church as their holy house.

To be safe in his earth lord's territory, a Chamulan must beg permission and pardon from the spirits of the

The true owners of the land
are the spirit 'earth lords.'
Crosses mark shrines where
the villagers pray to the
lords for pardon and grace.

Most Chamulans still wear
home-spun woollen clothes.
When a man becomes an
elder of the village, he
dyes his shirt black.

mountains and caves. He must offer them food in the form of incense and candles, and drink in the form of clear home-distilled rum, called *pos*. Generous sustenance of the spirits does not go unrewarded: every house, every waterhole, every sheep pen, every cornfield, and today every school or road, is a present from the earth spirits in exchange for the humble gifts of respectful men. Meanness with gifts will be met with disaster: the school will collapse, or someone will drown in the waterhole.

Chamulans believe all men should work for what they own. Poverty is not regarded compassionately as hard luck (although it very well could be) but as the just result of extreme laziness: the very poor are suspect. So too are the very rich who must surely have used immoral supernatural means – bribery of the earth lords or the sale of other men's souls – to amass such a fortune. Savage gossip discourages show of wealth, which might also provoke witchcraft by people who envy it. The wise, well-behaved Chamulan owns only a little.

Their dress is still mostly woollen, spun and woven by the women who make all the clothes, from baby-wear to the elders' tunics. Unlike the white belted tunic which any boy or a man may wear, the elders' tunics are dyed black. Women wear long skirts and shawls with which they cover their faces before strangers. A young girl's attire is of natural undyed wool, but at marriage the natural color of the skirt disappears into black dye. As women age, their blouses too are blackened until only their red tassels and belts brighten the somber ensemble. Celebrants of saints' cults and civil officials wear ritual costumes, the men in black tunics or red suits and ribboned straw hats, while the women wear long, loose black blouses, heavily beaded and ribboned necklaces, and a wool head-covering. Chamulans like to dress in red and green-blue – two colors sacred to the Maya.

Chamulan marriages are usually between people of equal wealth. The boy (of 16 to 20) begs for a young girl (of 14 to 18) and supplies money, gifts, three days' manual labor and a nocturnal wedding feast to her parents. The young couple try to set up their own home near the groom's family-compound. Outside the circle of blood relatives, close friendships are rare so a lonely young wife often visits her family, who defend her in marital crisis. Divorce does occur – men leave lazy women, women escape drunken, cruel husbands – but marriages are usually long lasting.

According to their ideal – which is rarely fulfilled – Chamulans are chaste before marriage and faithful after it. Ribald jokes abound in private but decorum decrees that they should never be shared by both sexes. Decorum is particularly valued in public places: embarrassment gives Chamulans stomach-ache. All a Chamulan need say of a person he disapproves of is 'he doesn't know how to be ashamed.' People who express physical affection in public are deplored as lustful, crazy people.

At the birth of a child – a gift from god – a midwife and the husband both assist while relations gather round the mother with sympathetic encouragement. The new-born child is wrapped and bathed in purifying herbal waters and, to protect the mother's fertility, the umbilical cord and after-birth are ritually buried. The child, called a little monkey until it has been baptised, is pampered, particularly if it is a boy. When the next baby comes, the child's spoiling ends abruptly and he often plunges into a deep depression – which is generally ignored.

In Chamula, both sons and daughters inherit land and goods. Death – 'the time to be eaten by worms' – is almost always attributed to murder by witchcraft. There is great sorrow when parents die. Even a middle-aged man considers himself an orphan when bereaved.

Members of the immediate family may not prepare or bury the body. Elder relatives undertake this task in return for *pos* and food. The body is washed and dressed in finest clothes with a rosary across the chest; it is given small, burned *tortillas* and water for food in afterlife, lulled by music and quickly buried. No one is sure what lies ahead for the dead man: afterlife is oblivion. Stories told of a three day punishment in a hell called 'burning bones' and of an eventual reincarnation are not always believed.

Ancient Maya myth has evolved alongside Catholic dogma in Chamulan beliefs. Elders recount how the sun god Jesus Christ, called Htotik ('our Father'), and his mother, Mary, the moon, called Hme7tik* ('our Mother') lived on the earth. Htotik had created a crude, barbarous lot of people who eventually killed him on the cross with the aid of fierce half-man, half-animal demons called *pukuh*. They drove him and his mother into heaven. Htotik tried to create good people, but each of his four creations produced nothing but cannibals and sinners who perished at his anger or were turned into monkeys or squirrels as they fled his wrathful floods and burning rains. Today Htotik and Hme7tik receive prayers from the earth spirits 'Father' San Juan and his holy companions in the church. The kindly earth spirit saints point out the Chamulans' virtues and protect them against the disapproval of Htotik in heaven. As Chamulans sense uneasily that another cataclysmic destruction may be in the air, they express dismay at their companions' incessant wrongdoings: though quick to smile and joke with friends, the Chamulan has a pessimistic view of human nature.

At the center of Chamulan belief is the sun, the essence of life. The heat and light of the sun mean growth, health and fertility. Day is life; night is danger and death. People's souls contain spiritual heat. This is feeble at birth, but gradually warms with age until at old age people are strong and hot. Hottest of all are old but vigorous men: men are always hotter than women.

These principles of light and heat are governed by **99**

---

*7 represents the 'click' sound in the Chamulan language.

Chamulans still follow the beliefs of their famous Maya ancestors. The harvest which they discuss here depends on their spiritual goodness.

balance. The sun and moon need each other: cool rain, sleep, females and level-headedness are as essential to life and well-being as sunlight, activity, males and valor. Too hot a soul is dangerous for it drives its owner to quarrelling and witchcraft.

The municipal government relies on the power invested in the senior men to keep order and lead the community. Each Chiapan Indian municipio is autonomous. A municipal president is chosen by the Mexican politicians and elders of the municipio. Formerly, the president was a respected elder, but today each Indian president must be able to read and write Spanish, so younger men often take the post. The Chamula president is assisted by 68 elders, who carry the burden – or the cargo – of responsibility. Scholars call this political set-up the cargo system. Each important cargo-holder is imbued with strength

and prestige and carries the symbol of his office in a silver-tipped baton tucked under his arm.

San Juan also carries a baton, all silver, decorated with peacock and parrot feathers very like the quetzal-bird feather of the ancient Maya leaders. Chamulans celebrate him and all the saints who line the church – the male saints on the north side and the females on the south – and San Juan, who is president of the saints, thanks them with good crops and health. Should he be insulted by half-hearted generosity or sin, he is quick to get Htotik in heaven to send a plague, crop failure, or other suitable disaster.

People converge in Chamula Center to relax from their work and at fiesta time. Here they shop, drink, pray and rest their hearts. The cargo-holders dance day and night to the sacred harp and the guitar, singing to the saints or keeping everybody awake with the comic song of the jaguar – the *bolomcon*. They decorate the holy shrines with flowers of crimson – a color sacred to the Maya. They offer candles and incense, explode skyrockets and parade the saints around the churchyard.

The fiestas culminate in a Maya celebration called 'the Playing' corresponding to the five 'lost' days at the end of every 20-day month in the Maya calendar – when the cargo-holders, waving flowered flags, hurtle from shrine to shrine, escorted by men dressed as 19th-century soldiers, but called monkeys. As each part of the fiesta is a gesture to prove man's worth despite his sinful nature, the cargo-holders' behavior must be perfect. They give away prodigious quantities of food and perform the obligatory rites – the dance upon the sacred pots, the running through fire, and even the horse-dung fight on the last day – and they do all this willingly and without rancor.

Yet the cargo-holders have enemies. These are witches of either sex, each with a fiery soul and greedy, lascivious, hot-headed, cruel and irresponsible. The witch is called to this wickedness through a dream sent by the cave-dwelling *pukuh*. Although young, the witch soul is strong and from an early age knows how to destroy the more pacific souls of his fellow Chamulans. Whereas the cargo-holder surrenders his wealth to maintain harmony, the witch burns one or two small candles upside down in a cave to wreak havoc, misery and illness upon his fellow men. Jaguars and coyotes are the animal soul companions of witches. Crucifixes on houses protect the dwellers from witches and *pukuh*; the cross deflects the power of evil.

How long will the Chamulans remain culturally intact? Today, non-Chamulans may not enter the church, and tourists with cameras are thrown into jail for taking the odious pictures which steal men's souls. Chamulans are trying to preserve their cultural identity in an unstable world where people say that penicillin is better than *pos*, where microbes, not witchcraft, cause illness, where children should go to school, not fiestas and cornfields, where men and women must learn Spanish, not just *Tzotzil*. The Chamulans move cautiously into modern Mexico, preserving their Maya heritage which gives them their strength, vitality and uniqueness.

Poverty in Chamula is always attributed to laziness or disrespect for the gods, which will justly lead to punishment on earth.

At festivals 'cargo-holders' sing and dance all night. They keep the players awake with the comic song of the evil jaguar.

Black peoples of Mexico and Central America

Descendants of the Black Caribs recall one item of their strange history by re-enacting annually their landing in British Honduras.

In the fifteen years following Columbus' arrival on the mainland of Central America in 1502, Spanish ships ferried the unfortunate indigenous people, erroneously identified as Indians by Columbus, from the Bay Islands in the Gulf of Honduras to Cuba as slave-labor. This was to characterize the white man's impact on the entire area for more than three centuries.

The Indians proved unsatisfactory slaves. In 1524, three years after Cortés destroyed the Aztec capital Tenochtitlan and replaced it with Mexico City, Gil González de Avila, missionary, explorer, and a high-minded man, arrived in what is now the Republic of Honduras bringing with him the answer to the slave problem. He was accompanied not only by the first Spanish woman ever to set foot on Central American soil, but also by some Africans.

Labor was scarce in Central America. Slavery was essential, it seemed, to the development of the new Spanish empire. That first trickle of Africans developed into a flood. During the century that followed possibly more Africans than Europeans came to the Central American isthmus. The slaves were brought mostly to Honduras from where they were distributed into Nicaragua, El Salvador and Guatemala. During that first century they were a distinct, large component of the Central American population. But progressively they lost both their status as slaves and their corporate identity. Long before the statutory abolition of slavery in 1824 many of the negro slaves had become free men – either by desertion or by formal individual liberation – and the negroes had melted into the general population. For example, of the total population of over a million that lived under the Spanish Audiencia de Guatemala at that time well over half were Indians; pure-bred Spaniards, though dominant, were few; and most of the remainder were *meztizos* or mulattos, people of mixed blood.

Today half the population of the Central American isthmus are of three groups of more or less pure descent: Indians – which are the vast majority – Europeans and a tiny minority of negroes. The other half are people of mixed descent, in varying combinations, from the three original groups. Here, too, the Indian element predominates.

In the Republic of Honduras and in Nicaragua many English-speaking negroes from the British West Indies have added to the basic racial mix of two Africans and one European to every seven Indians. In Guatemala there are black groups living in the lowlands on the Pacific and Caribbean coasts, but very few in the highlands. In El Salvador, which is densely populated, the negroes are wholly assimilated and hardly distinguishable as a separate group in the total population. In Costa Rica where 97 per cent of the inhabitants are white, only half of one per cent are Indian; the 2 per cent of the population who are of African origin are concentrated in the province of Limón where they represent 103

Black peoples of Mexico and Central America

Fishermen punt down the
Belize River with a precious
cargo of lobsters which
are all exported to
the US.

one-third of the population. At present the minority of people in Central America who are predominantly negro, although still racially more or less distinct, have been culturally assimilated into the life of the countries in which they live.

Most of these peoples whose origins are mainly or completely African are distinguishable only by their physical appearance. Either they have assimilated the predominantly Spanish language and culture of the isthmus or, as in the Bay Islands where there has been an influx of negroes from the British West Indies, black and white people alike are Protestant and English-speaking.

There is one interesting exception: the people known as the Black Caribs. They live in about 25 settlements scattered in three countries along four hundred miles of the coastline of the Gulf of Honduras. In the Republic of Honduras the citizens of the town of Trujillo are nearly all Black Caribs as are almost the entire populations of about 15 villages. In Guatemala they are a majority in one village and in the town of Livingston. In the colony of British Honduras they are a majority in the towns of Stann Creek, Punta Gorda and in three villages. There are also a few widely scattered groups in Yucatan to the north and in Costa Rica to the south, and a larger settlement at Pearl Lagoon in Nicaragua.

West African rhythms reverberate along the coast of Honduras, where Black Caribs have preserved a racial and cultural identity.

The history of the Black Caribs is curious: it illustrates how shared experience can weld together people of diverse origin. Slaves brought in by the British and Spanish often escaped or were liberated; others found unexpected freedom as survivors of shipwrecks. Early in the 17th century, many of these free Africans settled in the island of St Vincent. They came largely from the Caribbean islands to windward in boats and rafts. On St Vincent, which is 1,800 miles from the coastline of the Gulf of Honduras where they now live, they encountered the Island Caribs, a local Indian people, neolithic in culture, who spoke a modified Arawak language. Later in the 17th century Colonel Stapleton, deputy Governor of Antigua, wrote in a letter that there were 'about 1,500 Indians in St Vincent, St Lucia and Dominica; 600 of these bowmen are negroes, some run away from Barbados and elsewhere.' Two distinct races began to merge.

Despite their reputation for ferocity and cannibalism, the Island Caribs were simple and vulnerable and soon found themselves dominated and even oppressed by the African newcomers. The Africans for their part had good reason to assume the way of life and the culture of the Island Caribs: they had to survive in an environment the Caribs were accustomed to and they were not. Moreover there was less risk of enslavement for them among the Indians. Though they came from many different parts of West Africa, they achieved a unity of their own by adopting the culture and language of the island.

In 1763 St Vincent was annexed to Great Britain by the Treaty of Paris. During the following years – and especially during the American Revolution – the Black Caribs gave the British authorities a great deal of trouble. They staged two separate rebellions with French help and were subdued only with difficulty. By this time they were some five thousand strong while the white population of St Vincent, which numbered only about one thousand, regarded them as untrustworthy and not to be tolerated as neighbors. In 1797, they were deported *en bloc* to the island of Roatán off the coast of Honduras, and left there.

There is still a single Black Carib village on Roatán, but most of the deportees stayed only a short time on the island. Some crossed to the mainland at the invitation of the Spanish governor, and became established on the coast near Trujillo, which is still their 'capital.' Some served as soldiers under the Spanish flag; others fled to the Mosquito Coast to avoid this fate. Many joined the royalist forces in their unsuccessful attempt to overthrow the republican government of Honduras in 1832: it was probably a group of refugees escaping northwards who reached British Honduras after this defeat that founded the first Black Carib settlement there at Stann Creek.

They are a coastal people who live primarily by fishing. This is still mainly for home consumption, although in recent years refrigerated ships from the USA have patrolled the coasts, buying fish direct from the boats at sea. The Black Caribs fish with hook and line, nets, harpoons and with basketry fish traps, made locally from arrow-reed. There is also some small-scale horticulture, each household having at least one, usually several, *manioc* fields. This plant, which is their chief crop, produces tubers like potatoes, which are grated and dried to make meal: from this meal they bake the flat brittle cake, cassava. Their family life is stable, though it has changed in recent years, as the father must often seek employment away from home and leave his wife and children for long periods. They have an informal attitude to marriage: many unions are only blessed by church and state after many years and some not at all. This involves no social or moral stigma. Their sexual morals are strict; the Black Carib girl is said to be much less accessible than her creole or *ladino* neighbors. The would-be seducer is likely to be beaten up. Even in the town of Belize – the capital of British Honduras – there is little prostitution.

Carib and African respect for their ancestors as purveyors of the life force, and consequently the need of the living to bear children, co-exists without apparent strain with a loose and syncretic Catholicism. Ancestors are all-important: their messages are interpreted by the priestly functionary or shaman known as a *buiai*. The *buiai* enters a trance to receive his messages. In response to their ancestors' requests, Black Caribs perform long elaborate improvised rituals in a state of high fervor. Not only do they worship the Christian God and honor the spirits of their ancestors; they are also anxiously aware of being surrounded and often threatened – sexually and otherwise – by supernatural beings from whom they must protect themselves by complex rituals.

They are, however, a cheerful, forward-looking people, conscious of the value of education with a profound interest in their past, and a concern for their future. Among the black peoples of Central America, they alone retain a defined and separate identity: a blend of African race and Indian culture.

105

The mystery of Guatemala

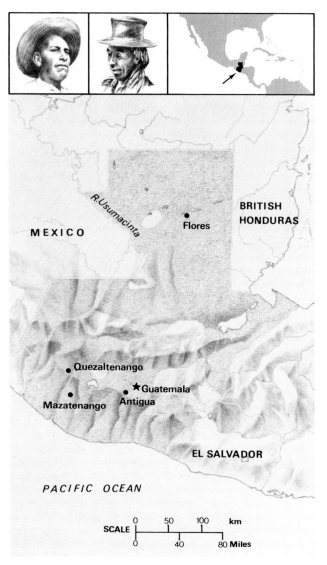

Guatemala is an ancient and venerable land, where nature and history have left majestic signs of their shaping power. Of all countries it is without doubt one of the richest in mysteries and inexpressible secrets, and not only in Central America, this fabulous Carib mediterranean, navel and sanctuary of the ancient Indo-American cultures.

I think that my work, as a novelist and poet, can also be interpreted as an unceasing celebration and vindication of the beauty of Guatemala, of aspects that are both remote and everyday, of its people and its customs. My work has been an attempt – perhaps not deliberate and conscious but deeply authentic – to recuperate and relive, in harmony, all the roots of our history and all its episodes.

To speak with justice about Guatemala one would have to be at one and the same time a geographer and a

An Indian market overflows
the steps of Chichicastenango
church, taken over by the
Maya-Quiche for their own
religious rituals.

People of Guatemala

*There are more than five million people in Guatemala and
of these 67 per cent are pure Indian - the highest
proportion of pure Indians in any country in Central
America. Guatemalan Indians live mainly in the
mountainous western part of the country and are
descended from the Maya, whose brilliant and melancholy
civilization once extended over the whole Yucatan
peninsula. But about 900 AD their civilization dissolved
leaving little but ruined cities and records of their
dramatic achievements in mathematics and astronomy.
The Indians of today seem to live in a world that has
barely changed; in the mountains, their villages are
self-governing and, because of difficult communications
in that harsh country, self-supporting. There is, of course,
industry in Guatemala. But this is more the concern of
the mestizos, the Spanish-Americans, and takes the form
of plantation farming which produces cheap fruit and
raw materials for the US. Less than 200 European and
mestizo families own 98 per cent of the fertile land.
Prosperity and the control of government come to the
50,000 white Europeans—mostly Spanish and German—
more easily than to any of the other peoples of
Guatemala. It is a country of wide differences; a beautiful
country, ulcerated by twenty or more volcanoes.
Conflict, sudden death and smouldering rebellion are
always near the surface in Guatemala.*

Boys in the streets of San
Pedro Sacatapeqez watch an
impromptu cock-fight.
Nearby is an Indian school
for training the birds.

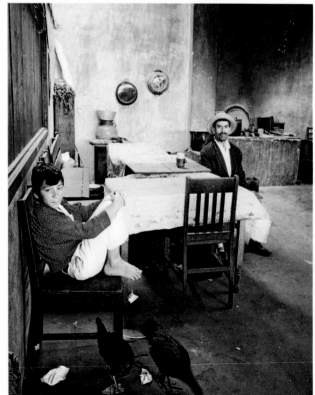

A restaurateur in San Pedro
Sacatapeqez serves the basic
tortillas and *enchilladas*
and rice and beans — but
with a flourish.

Christian Indians in San
Andres celebrate the
Easter festival. Here
they parade huge effigies
of Jesus and Judas.

Scenes like this encourage
guerrilla movements against
what followers see as
overfed oligarchies and
US economic tutelage.

historian, an archaeologist and a botanist, an anthropologist and a poet. Rather than attempt to include everything, I shall try to give the reader not so much an image of Guatemala as my own image of Guatemala, the mystical country of my heart, whose undying golden light illuminates my European evenings.

I shall begin with the light, the light of Guatemala. There where the landscape is bluest, a succession of scenes unveil themselves before us, changing in the distance from dark green to the bluish waves of a mountain range which turns into sky. This is no metaphor. Here metaphors are useless; reality surpasses them, they sound outworn and spent. Metaphors are not made by the writer or the poet but by nature.

Later on the light becomes golden, transparently golden, rather like the light in Cuzco. It doesn't shine onto us. It floods into us, entering not only through the eyes but through the pores. There's a feeling of drunkenness, of joy, of complete health in mind and body. One forgets everything apart from this sensation of supreme grace, of absolute euphoria. The road passes through giant clusters of pines, pines which rise from the depths and sloping walls of enormous gorges and thrust forth their dark green tinged with blue, in contrast with the other shades of green of the common plants and bushes. In the sticky patches under their ancient branches that

sway in the wind there are orchids and parasites with capricious shapes. The sound of voices, the noise of the engine and of the straining wheels deepen the silence which, as we go up, envelops everything, taking us away from the world to bring us back to ourselves.

In something less than two hundred and eighty kilometers one can travel through all the climates, all the landscapes, and all the countries that these scenes remind us of. From the Black Forest, to the forests of the Tyrol, from Florentine scenery to the South of France, from the flat stretches beside the roads in the Pyrenees to the peaks of the Alps. It can't be imagined unless one sees it. Below, at the foot of the valleys, as though resting on trays of jade, tiny villages - church, bridge, little houses - can be seen, and all this landscape is full of Indians dressed in their regional styles, like Assyrian gods. Clouds, and water in lakes, pools and pleasant rivers. Someone points . . . but there's no time to focus one's eyes, because one's attention has already been caught by something else. It's best to enjoy this landscape not for its details but in its entirety, for its display of vibrant profusion.

One is taken up and then down by roads that curl round like snakes. Could this enforced twisting between hills and mountains, valleys and gorges have helped make the snake a sacred symbol? Are not these roads 109

Miguel Angel Asturias **Mystery of Guatemala**

Guatemalan love of color means that nothing stays plain that can be decorated. This photographer's backcloth is a primitive painting.

Close-cropped hair for young men is *de rigueur* in Guatemala. Otherwise you are suspected of sympathy with the guerrillas.

the ciphers of the plumed serpent? The new asphalt roads have unfortunately left aside the little villages which were reached by the old earth roads and which men now only dream of.

These high regions were the home of the Maya, the primitive inhabitants of these enchanted lands. Here maize was born, for the first time in the world. And the tribes set off from here when they emigrated to the plains, not without leaving behind vestiges as important as the ruins of Zaculeo whose whiteness, the result of a disastrous attempt at reconstruction, can be seen from the Cuchumatanos in the immense expanse of blue, green and gold.

Nothing is left. On the sandy floor of an abandoned mine there are tiny snails and sea-shells. Some people claim that these heights were once covered by the sea. The idyllic atmosphere takes charge once again; one stops thinking and gives oneself to a sensual immersion in this world of magic, the fitting cradle of the Maya artists, the Maya sages, the Maya farmers, the Maya astronomers. . . . One must smell the air: the eyes are not enough to take in all the richness of this world. One opens one's arms to clasp this intangible space: it is not enough to smell the perfume of immensity and centuries. I feel that I can even taste the flavor of the first grains of maize that were harvested here by dark hands like my own. . . .

With its profusion of climates, Guatemala is enormously varied in a geographical and horizontal sense. But in a historical and vertical sense it has an amazing complexity that is equally rich and varied. Guatemala is a country made up of buried, superimposed cities, like the floors in a tall building. Floor upon floor, city upon city. A book of old prints, bound in stone and with pages made of gold from the Indies, Spanish parchment and republican paper. A chest which encloses the frozen figures of a dead illusion, the gold from the mines and the moon's white hairs preserved in silver rings. Within the high city the ancient cities are preserved intact. Up the stairs there rise images from a dream, leaving no trace and making no sound. To pass from one door to another is to leave one century and enter another. Shadows flutter in the light from the windows. Ghosts are the words of eternity.

Everything is superimposed. Pyramids stand on top of pyramids. Over sculpted gods there are showers of hieroglyphs. Here in these ancient carvings lives the art of transmuting stone, the exhalation of dreams. Everything is superimposed. The language and its cadences. One feels sure that these mineral forms are growing. But the inexperienced eye is mistaken: there's a stiffness of death beneath all these living things. Here are the finest species of the animal kingdom, and the finest birds: the quetzal, and the cenzontle whose throat can utter the whole gamut of musical sounds. There are butterflies too, with their orchid wings, and reptiles with their

The Indians' *Conquista*
dance yearly dramatizes
their subjection to Spain.
Today police scrutinize
modern interpretations.

Guatemala is invariably
fraught with tension.
The faces of loiterers
betray anxiety markedly
tinged with cynicism.

111

Miguel Angel Asturias **Mystery of Guatemala**

Well-mannered ladies of the town await male attention outside their premises in the Guatemalan city of Esquintla.

Maoist, Fidelist, orthodox Communist or loyal citizen — which is he? In violent Guatemala a sensible youth keeps his beliefs quiet.

Over half the population of Guatemala is unemployed. Shoe shine boys like these keep alive (and equipped) on 15 cents (or six pence) a day.

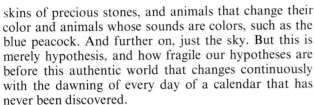

(Top) Dead drunkenness is common and within reach if three cents can be afforded for a bottle of *guaro*.

skins of precious stones, and animals that change their color and animals whose sounds are colors, such as the blue peacock. And further on, just the sky. But this is merely hypothesis, and how fragile our hypotheses are before this authentic world that changes continuously with the dawning of every day of a calendar that has never been discovered.

It is a calendar which moves with the rhythm of a walking man, as in the fable where time walks with the steps of man. Natural, logical, real and yet inhabitants of worlds with other categories, the Indians of Guatemala remind one of religious images, embroidered, sculpted, painted, brocaded. These Maya who have survived from past suns and not this moving sun come and go along the paths of Guatemala, possessors of some indefinable immortality. They are immortal in the same way that one is always there to replace the other at the market stall. When they talk they let forth a stream of words like a flock of birds. The magnificence of the women's dresses is a prolongation of the color of fruits. Everything is done without hurry. Time belongs to them. When they offer you their goods their hands go in and out of volcanoes of golden grain, clouds of fragrant tamarinds, round peppers black as night, round tablets of chocolate stamped with decorations, and turpentine ointments and medicinal herbs. As they return to the mountain paths, they are tall and ceremonious, dispossessed masters who wait for the return of the green fire.

They lost it because it was taken away from them. They were robbed of the green fire and there was nothing but anguish in the world. The moisture dried up and distances could no longer be spanned. Each man died where he was. The jungle turned into dust, mere dust between the fingers. And the sandy waste, and stones and the stifling air. Spiny fingers, long spiny fingers. Telescopes were made from the trunks of hollowed palms, to pierce the sky and reach up to the heights to ask the stars for the return of the green fire. When that day arrives what other hands have robbed will be theirs again. The Maya of Guatemala were robbed of the green fire, the crops that belonged to them, and this is why their books speak of the explosion of insatiable thirst. All was not said in the language of the water and the wind. The tarry sediment of the crystallized vegetation keeps alive the memory of that thirst and of the cries of those people, who are also these who come and go on the roads and in the villages, streets and plazas of Guatemala.

Cities. Other cities – newer, though still centuries old. Two-headed eagles, a plague of grotesque ornamentation and theologies. A religion of the catacombs could not be transplanted to a land of luminous festivals. Poor Spain. She took away a vacuum converted into gold, and left a tradition of blood and a sensibility which flourished in the crosses and swords over cities as ancient as this city of Old Guatemala, noisy and

alarming.

Immortal realm. The stars have returned to their places and the closing of the door of heaven has been signalled by a comet. The enigma remains, the enigma of the same repeated pattern that winds like a snake through churches, palaces and mansions. Monotony is worse than emptiness. So let's break it by getting drunk, let's make the walls drunk with the most fantastic decorations. Not out of 'fear of the void' but through the horror of boredom. Friezes, lintels, serrated trimmings. But we must pause here. Between the grain of maize and the sun begins the reality of dreams that have turned to ashes.

Guatemala is similar only to itself. Its mysterious presences and absences, all that's kept silent by the enigma. One doesn't have to read the hieroglyphs: one can read the stars. The blue hurricane has not returned from the ages. It will return, and then epochs and styles, messages and legends will be communicated to us. Meanwhile, let us enjoy this Guatemala of colors, this universe of green, wounded by the first flint that fell from the stars.

(Bottom) Coca-Cola is not always accompanied by US wealth. In Puerto Barrios, a bedraggled Caribbean Venice, canals are oily ditches.

Cuna
Panama and Colombia

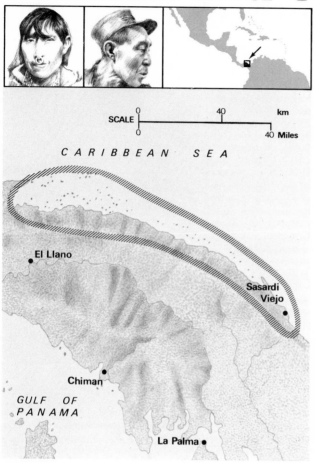

Amongst the tiny but myriad San Blas Islands just off the Caribbean coast of Panama live most of the 15,000 Cuna or *Tule* as they call themselves. Here and on the mainland in Panama and in Columbia they live blameless lives of quiet industriousness: fishing, weaving and making baskets. For all this the Cuna know that they will be rewarded: when they die they will go to heaven where all will be of gold and nobody will do any work at all. On the mainland their land is mountainous and, except for clearings made for building houses and planting crops, covered with dense jungle. But the islands are flat and so well populated that little of the forest is left.

The Cuna have not always lived in these parts. Some people think they are impoverished descendants of the Cueva Indians. At the time of the Spanish Conquest the Cueva certainly lived in some of what is now Cuna territory. But according to the legends of the Cuna and of their neighbors in the south, the Noanama Indians, the Cuna once came from Choco country on the Pacific coast of Colombia. The warlike Noanama had driven them first to the Rio Tiura area and the Cuna had sought refuge in the mountains of eastern Panama and the adjacent area of Colombia. They did not settle the San

These shamans have fulfilled the Cuna religious and social duty to drink and dance until no longer able to stand at an *inna* — a girl's coming of age.

Cuna Panama and Colombia

In Colombia Cuna territory overlaps with the Choco's — peace-loving people here crossing the Chucunaque river in a dugout canoe.

European origin, the Cuna live much as they have done for generations.

Fishing is still the basis of their economy. The Cuna who live on the mainland catch river fish with hook and line, spears and vegetable poison. Sometimes they trap fish by building dams into which the fish swim freely, but then find that the only exit, an ingenious wicker tube is too narrow to allow them to swim out again, and is anyway blocked by all the other fish that swim in. The Cuna who live on the islands go sea-fishing – sometimes whole families go off together in a boat. They catch the fish with nets.

Cuna men hunt, although less than they used to, with bow and arrow or shotgun. In much of Cuna country game is scarce, but it is often possible to catch peccary, armadillo, iguana, tortoises, frogs and various kinds of birds. A fortunate hunter will share his catch with his neighbors and relations. Meat and vegetables are stewed together in a pot. Sweet potatoes and cooking bananas are baked over the fire. Meat and fish are smoked or roasted over the fire. A visitor to a Cuna house is almost invariably welcomed with a plate of cooked food and a

Blas Islands until the 19th century.

The Cuna are proud of their descent and traditions. More successfully than many Amerindians they have resisted abrupt and sweeping changes even though Spanish, French and Scots settled alongside them on the Caribbean coast of Panama and they traded freely with British pirates in the 17th and 18th centuries, and despite the pressures of 20th century negro and white expansion in their once isolated areas. These contacts have subtly affected, but not entirely overwhelmed, their traditional way of life.

Many Cuna now have transistor radios. Some send their children to school in the towns or go there themselves to work or sell their produce. Occasionally a white missionary or doctor comes to live among them or a government official will pay them a visit. The Cuna use china, aluminium cooking pots and, on the San Blas Islands, motor boats. They have a particular fondness for telephone wires. They believe they are the means by which God keeps in touch with his people on earth.

But for these occasional intrusions, which are often so thoroughly incorporated into Cuna life that it is
116 difficult to tell whether they are of indigenous or

The island Cuna live off the yield of the sea — fishing, and diving for coins thrown from the tourist liners which anchor off the islands.

Life for the 15,000 Cuna on
their handful of islets (the
San Blas) is as nearly idyllic
an existence as the untutored
tropics can offer.

mug of unfermented beer made from maize.

In the Colombian settlements, strung out along a river for a mile or so, all the houses are out of sight, but within easy walking distance of each other along a broad, shady path. Each house is built well back from the river bank because of the frequent floods, but with a well-worn path that leads down to the water, for the Cuna spend much of their time by the river, fishing, bathing and washing their clothes. Each household has a number of gardens, some of which may be an hour's walk or more away from the house. On the San Blas Islands living is more cramped; most of the gardens are on the mainland, and the islanders rely more on fishing for subsistence.

Their houses are solidly built, rectangular structures 20 meters or more long and 4–5 meters high, with walls of wooden posts so that breeze and light can come in.

They are cool and airy in the tropical heat and, as the thatched roofs are coated with pitch, completely waterproof. In the cool twilight of the interior the feeling of spaciousness is emphasized by the simple furnishings – hammocks, used as beds by night and seats by day, and heavy wooden stools. When families are large, houses have one or more kitchens added on. Inside the kitchen is a hearth made of three tree trunks or thick branches. Their smouldering ends point inwards and provide fuel for cooking and support for the cooking pot.

The Cuna keep domestic animals best suited to forest life. They rear pigs, hens, ducks and turkeys mainly to sell to neighboring white people. They use dogs for hunting and have a few cats to keep down mice. Sometimes they rear young wild animals, particularly birds, as pets. In their clearings they grow bananas (especially the large cooking variety), maize, sugar cane and sweet

117

Cuna Panama and Colombia

Cuna boats sail off the
island of Carti. When canvas
is hard to come by, the
islanders improvise with
flour bags.

potatoes as well as tropical fruits such as pineapples, avocado pears, oranges, lemons and pawpaw. Some groups of Cuna cultivate cocoa, and coconuts are an important cash crop on the San Blas Islands. They sell other produce to whites and negroes when there is a surplus. The men work to clear the land but both men and women plant the crops. Weeding and harvesting are the women's jobs.

Cuna families tend to be large: parents, daughters and even grand-daughters marry and bring their husbands to join the group. Young families usually build a house of their own in their parents' compound, so that they can share house-work and care of the children. Once a man has sons-in-law he no longer has to work so hard since the sons-in-law are expected to work in his gardens as well as in their own. He has authority over his household, organizing the men of the family – both sons-in-law and unmarried sons – to work together in each of the gardens in turn. The members of the household, and indeed the whole community, normally address each other by a term of kinship – brother, sister and so forth – rather than by name.

Every Cuna daughter's life has three stages, each celebrated by a feast: when she is only a few months old and her septum is pierced to take a gold nose ring; at puberty; and when she marries. The first part of a feast

The appliqué work on this
grandmother's blouse is a
replica of the tattoos the Cuna
wore before the missionaries
forbade nudity.

118

is for eating. The second, when guests are summoned at around midnight by a blast of the conch shell from the village, and often the surrounding villages too, is for drinking fermented sugar-cane juice and for dancing. The villagers whirl in a horseshoe-shaped formation, back and forth at breath-taking speed in a blaze of color to the tunes of flutes and rattles. It is their religious and social duty to drink and dance until they can no longer stand steady on their feet.

The villages are kept in order by the chiefs and the police who are the chiefs' executives; their duties are to maintain paths and keep order during feasts. Chiefs are chosen by the community – for life, unless they commit grave misconduct. They need a thorough knowledge of Cuna traditions and enough Spanish to communicate with the national authorities. They keep order at village meetings by reprimanding misbehavers, reminding them of the punishment that awaits them after death on the path to heaven. Their misconduct could cause God to send floods and earthquakes. No further punishment is necessary. No names need even be mentioned: the culprit would rather mend his ways than risk a public shaming again: The chiefs give advice on good conduct

or sing long edifying songs of the life of the Cuna heroes, or *neles* (priests). They issue instructions about communal working parties. Attendance at village meetings, as at feasts, is attributed religious significance and the house in which the meeting is held is believed to be in direct contact with God by means of telephone wires.

The Cuna believe in one supreme God, the source of all goodness, who lives in heaven and justly punishes the evil and rewards the good. His rewards come as fair weather and the release of more game animals from the reserves in certain *kalus* – the mythical elaborate, many-storied buildings, complete with doors and windows, inhabited by other supernatural beings. *Kalus* are dangerous places where no ordinary mortal may go: on mountain tops, under the sea or in one of the different layers of the earth. Several Cuna have made drawings of them. Some spirits who live in these places are in effect God's bureaucracy, particularly in *Kalu Ibaki*, which is twelve stories high with offices, stools and tables inside where large numbers of people work. At *Kalu Ibaki* the workers receive instructions from heaven and information about world affairs. Other *Kalu* are inhabited by evil spirits, such as the *poni*, the spirits of

Every Cuna woman wears a gold nose ring. The first *conquistadores* thought they were on the trail of Eldorado when they saw the Cuna gold.

High religious intensity is the mood of priestly village shamans as they invoke the spiritual world with their Pipes of Pan.

119

At a girl's *inna* ceremony at puberty, her hair is cut short to mark her new status as an adult. Her companions cover their heads.

disease, who assume fantastic or animal form and come to Cuna houses to steal the inhabitants' *purba*, a vital force not unlike the Christian soul, without which a person will sicken and eventually die.

The *nele* is an intermediary between the mortal world and the spirit world, who has certain innate powers and more spirits at his disposal than ordinary mortals. He must be extremely well versed in Cuna traditions and beliefs learned from other *neles*. If things go wrong in a Cuna community, it is possible for a *nele* to set them right by making a journey to the appropriate *kalu*. When he goes to visit a *kalu* he takes four spirits with him and leaves four behind. By their good relations with evil spirits *neles* can also obtain knowledge of curing illness. However, not all *neles* always use their powers for the general good.

The *nuchus* are carved wooden figures and another link between the two world of the Cuna. Every household has about 50 of them, some eight inches high and clad in European dress of past centuries. The figures also have souls and can mediate between humans and malignant spirits, especially the ones which rob people's souls and cause illness and death. *Nuchus* will travel to the home of the spirits and wrest back the *purba* (the soul). When their help is needed, the *nuchus* are placed beneath the hammock of the sick man. A special functionary burns tobacco and cocoa and sings to the *nuchus*, suggesting what they should do to rescue the sick man's stolen soul: the burning smell is agreeable to the *nuchus*.

The Cuna believe that they go to heaven after death but that the journey there is long and dangerous. They are buried with half a calabash (gourd) over the head – to protect them from the woodpecker which might otherwise peck a hole in their skull – and with two ropes made in a special way so that they will expand to form a bridge over a large lake they must cross. A very sinful person will find that once in the middle of the lake the rope will contract to its original size and deposit him in the water, where a large animal will swallow him, regurgitate him on the shore he started from, to begin all over again.

Heaven, once you get there, is all of gold: clothes, buildings, game, boats, everything. There is no sun; even the light comes from the gold. No one is poor; no one must work. A replica of everything a person made on earth – boats, baskets, fish traps and so forth – awaits him in heaven. The same is true of each animal killed and of every present given. In heaven even sweeping is done by the wind.

The Cuna are excellent craftsmen and still make most of the things they use. Wood is one of their most important raw materials from which they make a wide range of items, from massive stools to cooking spoons with handsomely carved handles. They make baskets for storing and carrying things. Women bring huge bunches of bananas and other produce home from the gardens in what look like giant waste-paper baskets, supported

on their backs. In spite of the high standard of their basketry today, it seems to have deteriorated since the late 17th century when Lionel Wafer, an English ship's doctor, was forced to spend several months with the Cuna as the result of an accident. In his fascinating account of his visit, he mentions that the Cuna were such skilled craftsmen that they could make waterproof basketry drinking cups.

Only two items today are still woven: hammocks and headbands. Hammocks are of coarse home-spun cotton woven by women on a vertical loom. Although they take a long time to make and the Cuna can buy factory-made hammocks they prefer their own since only these are thick enough to prevent mosquitoes biting through from underneath.

Both hammocks and headbands have warp patterns. On the hammocks these are simple and improvised, many representing the markings on forest birds. The pattern on the headbands is more complex and is made with the help of pattern sticks. The same design is used on all the headbands but belongs to a group of patterns which the Cuna work on a wide variety of items, including appliqué blouses, fire fans, some baskets, bead bibs and ligatures. These designs represent plants and household implements, and occasionally animals.

The women are striking in their colorful appliqué blouses worn over wrap-around skirts of dark printed cotton. On their arms and legs they wear strings of colored beads of red, yellow and black, arranged in a pattern. Their thick black hair is long and loose to their waists in some areas – particularly the Colombian settlements – and cut short in others. Every woman or girl wears a small gold ring in her nose and a large number of necklaces of glass beads, shells, fish bones, palm nuts and other decorative materials. Men may wear monkey teeth necklaces. At village meetings and feasts, the women wear a red cotton scarf on their heads and both men and women rouge their cheeks with red *achiote* and paint designs on their faces with black *jagua*, which are thought to have a beneficial effect on the wearer's behavior. Nowadays men dress like any white or negro living in the area – in a pair of trousers and a shirt. The Cuna are an attractive people: they take great pride in their appearance and in the things they make. They have an extraordinary facility to absorb new ideas without allowing them to overwhelm their old beliefs which are complex and have not yet been properly studied. These beliefs are so much part of their everyday life that they are probably one of the secrets of their survival. They have also been helped until recently by their relative isolation. However, this is threatened not only by the ever-increasing number of white and negro settlers, but by the probability that the pan-American highway will be driven right through their area. It will be increasingly difficult for their present way of life to continue.

121

A Cuna woman removes the tough outer husk of coconuts, the Cuna's most lucrative crop, with big metal shears.

Peoples of Honduras and El Salvador

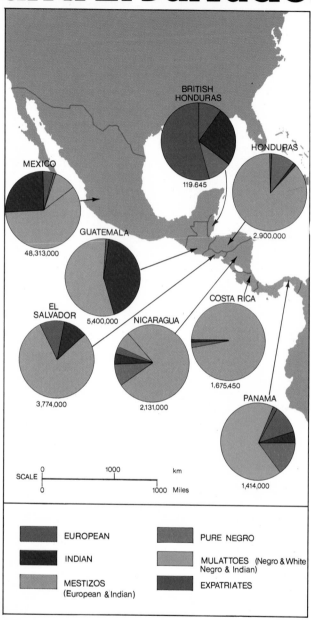

BRITISH
HONDURAS
119,645

MEXICO
48,313,000

HONDURAS
2,900,000

GUATEMALA

EL
SALVADOR
3,774,000

5,400,000

NICARAGUA
2,131,000

COSTA RICA
1,675,450

PANAMA
1,414,000

SCALE
0   1000   km
0   1000 Miles

EUROPEAN

INDIAN

MESTIZOS
(European & Indian)

PURE NEGRO

MULATTOES (Negro & White
Negro & Indian)

EXPATRIATES

In 1964, after a controversial football match, Hondurans
and Salvadoreans fell upon each other in a brief but
vicious little war. Yet an outsider might be excused for
thinking that Honduras and El Salvador would make a
happy couple. Their partnership could be founded on
many things—they are, for instance, close neighbors
and in their history they have shared many of the same
experiences. Both countries were formerly under the
Spanish colonial umbrella; both Hondurans and Salvadoreans have ancestors like the glorious Maya Indians,
the brilliant Aztecs and the peaceful Lenca. A partnership could bring together the large, thinly populated
country of Honduras with the small, densely peopled

122

LADO
B

The national anthem of
Honduras strikes up at the
end of the National Day
parade. Military and civilian
leaders stand to attention.

Peoples of Honduras and El Salvador

A common sight in San Salvador: the tiny coffin of an infant is lowered into the grave. There are only 22 doctors per 100,000 people.

country of El Salvador. The match, ideally, would seem to offer benefits to both sides. So why are there two countries? Why are their peoples at loggerheads?

The 'football war' was but another violent patch in a history that for both countries has been constantly chequered since they broke away from the Spanish Empire in the 19th century. By that time the people of the two countries were mostly of mixed Spanish-Indian (*mestizo*) blood and 300 years of colonial rule had submerged most of the ancient Indian cultures. But the threads that drew the two states apart, severing links they had shared under the Spanish, lay in the nature of the two countries. Development, prosperity and political unity came slowly for each country; and they also came at a different pace. While Honduras, soon after its independence, became a prototype 'banana republic' (in the phrase coined by an American journalist), with an economy dominated by the American United Fruit Company, Salvadoreans developed on a sounder, more self-sufficient basis. They were soon spreading unobtrusively across the border, homesteading on Honduran territory, but retaining their national allegiance. Here were the seeds of trouble.

El Salvador, guided by a group of 14 *mestizo* families, has been able to occupy and to develop most of its small territory. There has been a certain prosperity—

50 per cent of the people are literate—and the extremes of wealth and poverty are less acute than in other dictator-dominated countries. For Honduras there has never been much stability. The country is mostly mountainous and difficult to traverse. Poor communications make it difficult to market goods, encourage isolation and force small communities to grow crops entirely for their own consumption. One result of its plantation dominated economy has been to leave vast areas of the country underdeveloped and empty.

The early federation of these two states with others in Central America lasted from 1823 to 1838, until factionism and conflict between widely separated Indian communities and groups of *mestizo* landowners broke the bond. Sparse and scattered settlements throughout Central America never bred much co-operation between groups, except where there was a powerful and unassailable government; rather, the reverse was true. All the central American states, including Honduras and El Salvador, suffered from economic and government instability.

Yet behind this troubled history, for Honduras and El Salvador there lay a rich heritage of greater antiquity. From 300 AD the Maya civilization had dominated all of Central America. Maya were well versed in mathematics and astronomy, and they evolved a complex

124

Near Santa Tecla in El Salvador squatter shacks occupy public ground. The inhabitants are liable to be evicted at any moment.

numerical system and solar calendar. In the 14th century the Maya were eclipsed by the Aztec civilization, whose empire saw brilliant military achievements, the finest art and the cruellest religious rituals that pre-Columban America had ever witnessed. Only with the arrival of the Spaniards in the 16th century was the Aztec empire diminished and finally destroyed.

In Honduras and El Salvador, which lie at the southern extreme of the old Aztec empire, few of the other old Indian cultures survive. There are, for instance, only a thousand or so Paya and Jicaque who retain their old ways—and they do not do so out of choice. It is lack of alteratives in Honduras, rather than proud tradition, which causes these Indians to continue to hunt with blowpipes and bows and arrows; they grow a little maize and coffee (a plant brought to Central America in the early

Intensified farming in El Salvador has driven peasants off the land and into shanty towns. The urban population has doubled in ten years.

Peoples of Honduras and El Salvador

In Honduras special clinics have been set up to combat malnutrition. Younger children in large families at last have a chance to survive.

Workers in a Honduran match-factory listen intently as a social worker gives them a lecture on family planning.

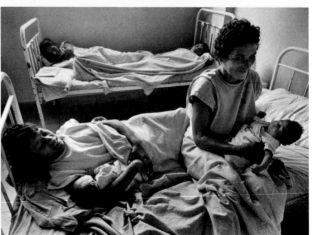

Adults acquire literacy at church centers in Honduras. The Church leads the fight for basic rights. Priests are often self-styled Marxists.

Back-street abortion is common in Salvador. In this overcrowded maternity ward, every fifth woman has come with an incomplete abortion.

in their resistance.

The Pipil Indians in El Salvador fiercely fought against the Spaniards. Almost half their numbers were killed before they were finally subdued. Between 1520 and 1590 an estimated 1,200,000 Lempa Indians in Honduras were reduced to 18,000. Lenca resistance lasted longer. Their villages had always been self-ruling; they were unused to a ruling class. They were stubborn, and a dozen years after the first conquest they rebelled again under a warrior named Lempira. The Hondurans of today recall his revolt with pride and have given his name to their currency.

Between 1522 and 1821 Indians who remained in their village communities were protected by the Spanish Crown, its agents and its priests, many of whom fought against the desire of some Spanish settlers to exploit the Indians. Despite regulations laid down by the Spanish Crown the Indians were, in fact, widely exploited. They were forced to pay tribute—payments of produce such as maize, honey and turkeys, and other traditional products like cotton—to the colonial government, to the church and to the settlers. They were also expected to work on the estates if required. This process of subjection, which took only a few years, was succeeded by a long-drawn-out process of assimilation of the two peoples. Soon separate *mestizo*, or *ladino*, villages were established and a few negro slaves, brought across from the Caribbean islands, were eventually merged with the *mestizo* population.

The majority of the population of Honduras and El Salvador today is *ladino*. Probably not more than 600,000 pure blooded Indians, living their old Indian life, still remain. But estimates that Indians are about 10 per cent of the population of Honduras and 5 to 20 per cent in El Salvador are misleading: Indians are not only a small minority; they also tend to be indistinguishable from the *ladino* majority.

Among the *ladinos* a little of the Indian culture lingers on, perhaps more in the mind than in any tangible, identifiable way of life. Among this entire group there is some memory of their Indian forefathers. They look upon their respective governments much as Indians regarded the Spaniards 400 years ago. If the government is both just and unassailable then it is best to respect it. If however, as has too often been the case, it is both unjust and assailable, then it is time to rebel: in El Salvador in 1832 and in 1932 the Indians were eager participants in rebellion.

The Indians share with *ladinos* an overwhelming sense of community and a low regard for marriage. In the past, in both Indian and *ladino* villages, the lands were communally owned. Each man had the right to cultivate, but not to own, the land. As both communities lacked private property, in neither did peasant values develop. Individuals strove neither for independence nor for personal wealth. A villager could not amass a fortune to pass on

19th century) and they practise a shifting agriculture as the land becomes drained of its nutrients. The slash-and-burn technique and their digging sticks are traditional methods of farming; they are also a symptom of their isolation from progress which has been made elsewhere.

Many Indian families live in the rocky hills. Once their homes were a sanctuary from the invading Spaniards, but now they are isolated. Their wooden, ox-drawn plows are practically useless on the rocky hillsides; their children grow up in straw huts where three stones on a dirt floor make a hearth, and narrow logs covered by a reed mat make a bed. The simplicity of their lives may be of interest and fascination to outsiders, but it is, nevertheless, a hard life. Four hundred years ago, to resist Spanish conquest, the Paya and Jicaque Indians took to the mountains—other Indian groups were less fortunate

127

Peoples of Honduras and El Salvador

Unemployment in Honduras and El Salvador is rife. These men are selling lottery tickets—a popular part-time occupation.

This Honduran laborer goes from estate to estate in search of casual work. He spends a month on this banana plantation, then moves on.

to his children; there was no such thing as a good financial marriage.

In fact, much to the displeasure of the Spanish priests, marriage has not become an important institution. It matters little if a couple stays together or separates. An unmarried mother is looked after by the community. The permanence of a marriage depends simply on the compatibility of the couple. It has always been so. Today as many as half the people take partners without the formality of a marriage ceremony. Not only girls but older women frequently have children without even living with the father. The church and the upper ranks of society disapprove of this family instability, but with little effect. To the Indians and the village *ladinos* it is the community that is important, the community that has the interests of the people at its heart. And this cannot be replaced by government.

On the old Spanish estates there was even less incentive to marry than in the villages, for estate workers were so dependent on their employers that a wife or husband could bring no greater security. The only way an estate worker could better himself was by proving himself to his employer by his loyalty as a servant, and by trying to establish friendly relations with him. Workers tended to distrust each other. Now they suspect anyone who

An ambitious US-financed project has meant a new education in farming and resettlement for these Honduran farm laborers.

talks of trade unions as either personally ambitious or the bosses' stooge.

After 1880 communal ownership of land was stopped in El Salvador. The land was to be divided among the villagers, each taking a plot for himself. In fact much of the land ended up in the hands of the more unscrupulous people who bought land from illiterate villagers at a fraction of its value. Even fewer people owned land than before. From communal ownership, land passed directly into the hands of the rich. Today less than a quarter of the farming people of El Salvador have title to their own land. Of these most have a plot so small that it is impossible to gain a living from it. The farming population was forced to become mobile. Many communities broke up—they no longer shared land, and nor could they remain in the same village the whole year round. Instead they went from one coffee plantation to another, sometimes renting land for a season then moving off to find a casual job.

There is still some communally owned village land in Honduras. Here the process of land-grabbing was more subtle. A man always had the squatter's right to settle on a new area and cultivate unclaimed land. But then someone with political influence would come along after him and claim the land as his own, and his squatter's rights

were blatantly ignored. Most of the better land passed into the hands of the vast estates and their wealthy owners. The rule of the rich was undeniable, though many more Hondurans than El Salvadoreans live off their own land today.

Right up to the 19th century Honduras largely ignored its Atlantic seaboard. Spanish governments merely built a few ports there and laid down a number of caravan routes. In the 19th century there was for a time an independent kingdom, called the Mosquito Coast, which existed with the sanction of the British Colonial office, populated by Mosquito and Sumo Indians and fugitives from other parts of Honduras. The Mosquito coast chiefs were educated in Jamaica. Today the remnants of the Mosquito and the Sumo tribes who once lived in the kingdom survive only obscurely in the marshes and jungles of eastern Honduras. There are probably no more than 15,000 left.

Here too are separate groups of poor English people and negroes. The 8,000 whites, many of whom are merchant seamen, speak English and do not inter-marry with the negroes. The atmosphere in their towns and villages is reminiscent of a mid-west American town of the last century. They have little choice but to remain where they are, selling their fish and coconuts to Hondurans, 129

Honduran army cadets stir the people. Patriotism is so strong that in 1969 a football match sparked off a war with neighboring El Salvador.

Trade unions have increased
their power in Honduras. They
organize good cheap housing
for some members — like this
delighted banana cutter.

Honduran policemen seem to
reflect the influence of
Wild West sheriffs. The power
of the local *jefe* (police
chief) is usually strong.

subjects of the Honduras government. Some feel deserted
by the mother country, resent their isolation from other
whites, and regret their great grandfathers' settlement
there in times of British authority and greater prosperity.

The negroes, descendants of the African slaves shipped
to the Caribbean islands for sugar plantation work, and
brought to this part of northern Honduras at the end of
the 18th century, speak a Caribbean language and do not
mingle easily with other Hondurans. They are scattered
all along the Atlantic coast of Central America and the
15,000 who live in Honduras make their living by fishing
in dug-out canoes while their women grow bitter yucca
(a plant of the lily family) as a staple crop. Many of the
Black Caribs have adopted *mestizo* ways; many are
Catholic and incongruously perform the dance play
Moors against the Christians, a popular event in small
town fiestas, brought by the Spanish to commemorate
the Moors' expulsion from Spain.

In both Honduras and El Salvador there are groups
and factions who do not easily mix; but there is also
assimilation. Spaniards and Indians were once poles
apart, but have now merged as *ladinos*. Within the two
countries the process continues, often in spite of the
barriers built up by governments wishing to exploit
grievances and prejudices.

131

Ancient Mexico and Central America

There are three broad cultural influences in modern Mexican society. There is the society that you see in and around the big cities: the factories, roads, cars, apartments, offices, airports and all the other manifestations of the universal late 20th century culture. Then there is the Latin and Catholic culture brought to the country with the Spanish Conquest of 1519, which is what predominates. Spanish is the language of Mexico and the Church is still influential. Culturally this is very much a Mediterranean land. But these are relatively recent influences, superimposed upon a third, more ancient, indigenous culture.

There remain about four million of the indigenous people, the inheritors of what was once a great and independent empire. The 'Indians' live mainly in the small villages and *rancherias* of the Mexican countryside, cultivating their corn and chili, beans and squash, practising the arts of the weaver and the potter very much as in the old days. They have certainly come under Spanish influences. But there was influence in the other direction too; and it is not possible to understand the life and culture of present-day Mexico, as a whole or in any aspect, without first seeking to understand the story of these indigenous people and their distinctive civilization.

In the history of the world, there have been few civilizations that were highly advanced and genuinely independent. This was one of them. We think of it, rather too loosely, as the Aztec civilization. The story of its ending is well known: the Emperor Moctezuma II, divine ruler of a rich society, proved too subtle and perhaps too gentle to cope with the better-armed aggressors from Spain.

The Aztecs' story needs to be placed, historically and geographically. It is necessary first to drop the word 'Mexico', with its suggestion of modern political frontiers, and speak instead of Mesoamerica ('middle America'). In a sense, this is a Mexican story, but it concerns a civilization which, although not covering the whole of modern Mexico, extended beyond its southern frontiers. Aztec territory ran from the Soto La Marina and Sinaloa rivers in northern Mexico, southward and eastward to the Gulf of Nicoya in Costa Rica and the Motagua River in Honduras.

The Aztecs were only the last of a whole series of cultures and empires that flourished and declined over a long period in Mesoamerica. Before them there were the Olmec, the Teotihuacan, the Toltec, the Huastec, the Totonac, the Tarascan, the Zapotec, the Mixtec, the Maya, and many others. Descendants of these civilizations survive today in varying numbers, their respective cultures distinguishable in the enormous variety of their buildings and artifacts. Still, Mesoamerica can be regarded as a single civilization. It has for example artistic unity: although Olmec sculpture may be very different from Maya sculpture, few Mesoamerican buildings or artifacts could be supposed to come from any other part of the world. And Mesoamerica had a religious unity. Throughout this large area and its long history people worshipped the same gods: the important God of Rain and Quetzalcoatl, the friendly God of Wind and Cultivation, and many others. Representations of these gods took many, often animal, forms, but their character and role are similar everywhere. While the various cultures and empires of Mesoamerica seem distinct in retrospect, there were continual military and commercial contacts between them and a high degree of cultural cross-pollination.

The story begins some 25,000 years ago, during the last glaciation, when a bridge of ice formed across the Bering Straits and enabled migrations of Mongoloid peoples to begin from Asia. They came in successive waves, initially over North America, then over Central and South America. For millennia these people lived as wanderers, by hunting and gathering and fishing; then, about 7,000 years ago, they began to live by agriculture and in settlements. By 2,500 BC the people of Mesoamerica lived in villages and did basket-work, weaving and pottery.

From these primitive beginnings, the civilization of Mesoamerica began around 1,400 BC with a people whom we now call the Olmec. Olmec means 'land of rubber' and is the later name of the place where they lived – the flat, humid, alluvial plain on the southern side of the great bay formed by the Yucatan peninsula and Central Mexico. Mounds still remain upon which their temples once stood – on a straight north-south line in accordance with their beliefs and ceremonies. Although the main pyramid at La Venta is nearly 100 feet high, their architecture appears to have been relatively primitive. But their sculpture was grand, monumental and abundant. There is little stone in the area: like the builders of Stonehenge, they brought it laboriously from far away. But they worked it locally with astonishing skill into colossal heads, altars, huge stelae – carved stone blocks – and sarcophagi.

The character of their sculpture suggests that the Olmec may have been humanistic by contrast with the more theocratic cultures of later Mesoamerica. For the later emphasis tends to be on dignity and religious symbolism, and on the priestly or royal significance of the human figure. The Olmec seemed to concentrate their attention upon the human body itself with a deep aesthetic and non-sexual interest in its postures and plains and surfaces. No bones survive from their period, and it is only from these sculptures and other artifacts, large and small, that we have to make what inferences we can about their personal appearance. It seems that they tattooed and ritually scarred themselves and filed their teeth – all of which are fairly universal practices. More characteristic of Mesoamerica is the practice – apparently already established of the time of the Olmec – of deforming and elongating the skull by bandaging in infancy.

The Olmec were a trading people. They may have used their distinctive and often beautiful works of art for trading purposes, since these are found all over Mesoamerica. But they were probably also a warlike people, pioneers in the routine of war and conquest and the exacting of tribute that became characteristic of Mesoamerican history. They seem to have had a limited empire which flourished from roughly 800 to 400 BC and then declined, perhaps because of the increasing tyranny of a priestly caste. This led to rebellion and then to social breakdown. Olmec influence continued, notably among the Zapotec in the south, but the Olmec society disappeared.

At the time of the Olmec decline, there were in the central Valley of Mexico scattered farming villages where in a crude form one of the characteristic arts of Mesoamerica was practised: the erection of mounds and later of pyramids for temples. And at some time between 200 BC and 150 AD these people began to concentrate upon a certain spot in the middle of the Valley where they built the two vast pyramids of the Sun and the Moon. And so, about forty miles to the north of Mexico City, was established the first and perhaps the greatest center of Mesoamerican culture, the city of Teotihuacan. Even today, ruined and deserted, it is impressive. Those two great pyramids still stand, oriented to the north and south points of the compass, though now without their original stucco coverings. Each has its plaza of smaller pyramids, the temples that once topped them now gone; and straight through the city runs a long avenue called the Street of the Dead, though it contains no tombs.

Teotihuacan must in its day have been a crowded and bustling city – the first real city of Mesoamerica. It had a large population, clearly differentiated into social classes and professional groupings; it had a great monumental art, less humanistic and more hieratic than that of the Olmec; and it had an economy that worked for centuries. Like that of the Olmec, the Teotihuacan economy almost certainly depended on war, tribute, and commerce, conducted on a more or less imperial basis. As in the later Aztec empire the people of Teotihuacan probably followed conquest of their neighbors with establishing a friendly puppet government over them, then regularly collected tribute under sanctions that may have been religious as well as military. Their manpower was deflected on a large scale from subsistence agriculture to industrial tasks, manufacturing countless articles for trade. Artifacts have been found at Teotihuacan from all other regions of Mesoamerica. The city was a two-way center of commerce, and probably also a center for pilgrimage.

It was at Teotihuacan that Mesoamerican civilization made its most remarkable scientific, astronomical, mathematical, and literary progress. Then around 650 AD the city began to decline: the arts and crafts became decadent, building dwindled and stopped, and the ruling priestly caste began to lose their power. Teotihuacan was too weak to withstand attacks of more primitive people who came, burning and looting and destroying, from the north like the Goths upon Rome. The immense ruins, which people would come expressly to marvel at, remained. But before long their origin – and the whole story and achievement of Teotihuacan – was forgotten. By the 14th century the Aztecs believed that the ruined city was actually the work of giants, a home of the gods, and the birthplace of the Sun in the most recent of its five incarnations. Visiting those ruins now, one can easily share the feeling that this is an incomprehensible and holy place – the feeling which drove the great Moctezuma II, during those last years before the Spanish Conquest, to make an annual pilgrimage there.

The invaders, the Toltec, who destroyed the city, took some of its culture upon themselves. The Toltec's great hero was the chief Quetzalcoatl, not to be confused with the ancient god whose name he took. In 980 AD he established himself at Tula, close to Teotihuacan and inherited much from that long-dead city and culture. His nineteen-year reign was a creative and brilliant period, marked by a change from a religious and priestly emphasis to civil and military matters. But the gods of Quetzalcoatl and the Toltec were not driven out or forgotten; they seem to have been more cruel and terrible than those of Teotihuacan.

Between the isthmus of Tehuantepec and the southeastern borders of Mexico, and on into what is now Guatemala and Honduras, the ancient and stable civilization of the Maya flourished over all these years. And Maya descendants still occupy the same country and speak various dialects of the same language. The first date ever recorded on the American continent was found on an Olmec site – it was 2nd September, 31 years before the birth of Christ. Three hundred years later the first Maya stele appears; Maya society was still flourishing under Aztec rule at the time of the Spanish Conquest. It was a rich culture, remarkable for many kinds of learning: astronomy and the calendar, hieroglyphic writing, and above all mathematics. The Maya used a vigesimal system of numbers represented by dots and bars, with a dot representing 1 and a bar representing 5. Zero was represented by a kind of shell, and it was the introduction of this concept – as in Europe and among the Arabs – which made real mathematics possible.

There were many other peoples within the civilization of Mesoamerica, and the story of their inter-related cultures is complicated and, in some respects, conjectural. It is chiefly told for us in their buildings and 133 artifacts, but also in actual documents, written in hieroglyphics on bark-cloth paper or deer skin. We would know more if so many documents had not disappeared in pre-Columbian times, during the Spanish viceroyalty and even as recently as the 19th century.

By the time the Spanish came, bringing the questionably beneficial civilization of Europe, the empire of the Aztecs – the original 'Mexico' – was at its height. Their story starts on curious and somewhat romantic lines. In some respects it resembles the first beginnings of the empire of Venice. The Aztecs, a small band of wanderers or semi-nomads with a tribal form of social organization and achievement, arrived in the central Valley of Mexico about 1215. Already they were notoriously ill-behaved and had been expelled from one place after another. After several more of these rejections, they took refuge in the last available place, a small marshy island in the Lake of Texcoco, later to become Mexico City, just as the first Venetians took refuge in their lagoon and their marshy island. And the resemblance continues, for both cities are today in danger of subsidence and flooding.

This settlement of refugees, founded in 1325, was then named Tenochtitlan. Within two hundred years, it developed into a subtle and complex society, the center of a loose but extensive empire, and a city whose splendor astonished the Spanish conquerors. Cortés gazed upon the palace of Moctezuma II and declared that there was nothing like it in Spain.

We see Tenochtitlan mostly through the eyes of its conquerors and destroyers – who were so efficient that not a single ancient monument survives within Mexico City. Even so, we can form a rough picture of this great city and society at its height. Its population was probably more than 200,000. The houses were mostly white, flat-roofed and low, for the marshy site would not carry too many large buildings, and only great men's houses were allowed to have two floors. But there were many vast pyramids and temples. The city was dominated by the immense double temple of Tlaloc (god of rain and vegetation) and Huitzilopochtli. The layout of the city was spacious, geometrical and impressive; there was no wheeled traffic, but there was heavy waterborne traffic on its many canals, and it was mostly by these means that the city's open and well-stocked markets were replenished. It seems that the Aztecs ate well: maize in various forms was the staple diet, with beans and many other vegetables and fruits. They had no cattle and therefore no beef, but for meat they had turkeys, rabbits and hares, deer, wild pigs, various wildfowl and a number of other dishes – crows, frogs, snails, insects and a kind of hairless dog that was bred specially for the pot. They knew tobacco and the social function of smoking, and like many other Mesoamericans, they used *peyotl* and certain mushrooms as trance-inducing drugs for religious purposes. They were far from being a per-

missive people. They were, in fact, puritanical about both alcohol and sex. Adultery was punishable by death, and so – in many cases – was public drunkenness although it was condoned in the old, who were supposed to be past any kind of responsibility, and could drink *pulque* – the fermented juice of the agave plant – freely.

Aztec life was varied by a number of festivals in which sport played a large part as it usually had religious and ceremonial associations. Their most celebrated game, called simply 'the ball game' by modern writers, was played on courts, found all over Mesoamerica, each shaped like a capital I: a long narrow rectangle, with a short transverse rectangle at each end. The ball was heavy and made of rubber, and the players tried by using only their knees and hips to get it to the opposing team's end of the court. There was a stone ring at each side, and to get the ball through one of these meant outright victory. It seems to have been sometimes like primitive football, with an element of basketball. Only the upper classes were allowed to play, bets were laid, and there is some suggestion that defeat may sometimes have meant ritual decapitation. The city, it seems, was well-governed; there was a strong sense of public duty, and severe punishment for corruption. Problems of water-supply, flood-control, and sewage-disposal were handled with remarkable efficiency.

In their early nomadic days the Aztecs had been an egalitarian society. But during their 200 years of city life it rapidly developed into an aristocratic and imperialist monarchy. Even so, it retained a certain democratic character. Every boy aspired and had the opportunity to be a warrior. If he did well, he could rise high in the state and in fortune. Honor and wealth were evidently given to men because they had distinguished themselves. So the ruling class was constantly renewing itself from below, and from the strongest and most energetic elements in the population. Alongside this essentially military aristocracy, there was an elaborate ecclesiastical structure, governed under the emperor by two equal high-priests of great dignity. Beneath them there was a hierarchy of priests and priestesses whose important duty was to serve the gods.

War and religion were the dominant themes in Aztec society. But at the time of the Spanish Conquest, a new mercantile class, as in Europe, was already beginning to gain power. The man who prospered in business tended also to rise socially and politically, but he had to move cautiously and with humility. From time to time, the military and religious establishments took sharp action against the ostentation of some careless merchant. It is interesting to speculate what would have happened if Tenochtitlan had been allowed to continue: probably the mercantile class would slowly have gained in assurance and power, but without becoming the dominant factor in the state.

134

At the lower end of the social scale, there were the common people, who were not entitled to own land except collectively and seem to have enjoyed a fair measure of well-being. Then, right at the bottom, were the slaves. But slavery was a relatively civilized institution among the Aztecs. The harsher version imposed by Spain aroused their strong moral disapproval.

There must have been a certain elegance and grace about life in Tenochtitlan. The Aztecs were a clean people – they even had a kind of sauna or Turkish bath, and dirtiness was either a self-imposed penance or a punishment. Their clothes and adornments were colorful, and more or less ornate – in accordance with the social position of the wearer. The higher ranks, and above all the emperor, must have presented a truly dazzling appearance.

The Aztecs were obsessed by the mysteries of death and blood, an obsession which together with much beauty and some wit, characterizes all Mesoamerican art. And they had a profound sense of doom and danger. They believed that the sun would cease its daily journeying, and so cause the end of all things, unless it were fed with human blood. So their life was centered around the necessity of sacrifice. Even war was sometimes ordered to this purpose. Its object was not to kill, nor even simple victory, but rather to take prisoners. (This is one of the reasons for the Spaniards' relatively easy victory: the two sides were fighting different kinds of war.)

Although the Aztecs were shocked by the tortures brought into their country from the land of the Inquisition, for them human sacrifice was not cruel: it was a necessary duty to ensure the continuity of life. This was also recognized by the victims, who were treated not as criminals but as honored messengers to the gods. Some seem to have accepted their fate, not only as a destiny with which they had been familiar from childhood and which guaranteed them a happy after-life, but as a privilege. The warrior who fell in battle went to a kind of heaven, but so did the man who was taken prisoner and led up the stone steps to where the priest would be waiting with his stone knife. For most other people, with some curious exceptions – women who had died in childbirth, for example, or men who had drowned – the next world held only a dreary and shadowy prospect. To be stretched out on that slab was to achieve both greatness and hope; and to the doom-laden mind of Mesoamerica, hope was a rare privilege.

Tenochtitlan fell, literally, and the distinctive Aztec culture was dispersed. But the Mesoamerica of the old days still continues, its religious legacy sharply modifying the Catholicism of the 'Indians', its social patterns not wholly submerged in those of Spanish and modern Mexico, so that this country is quite unlike any other, even in Latin America.

Glossary Peoples of Mexico and Central America

At least 90 per cent of the people in Mexico and Central America are mestizos: *descendants of unions between Spanish conquistadors and Indians. The* mestizos *adopted the Catholic religion and Spanish way of life and today occupy every sphere of political and economic life. Today the Indians represent about 8 per cent of the total population. The other 2 per cent include Spaniards, many of whom are refugees from the Civil War, negroes, Black Caribs, mulattos and the descendants of every possible mixture of these groups.*

INDIANS

The ancestors of the American Indian are believed to have entered the New World between 10,000 and 20,000 years ago towards the end of the Pleistocene. Evidence indicates that they came from eastern Asia via the Bering Straits. Certainly today the American Indians show Mongoloid characteristics, yet there are many physical differences between the Indian groups. The face of the middle American Indian is less flat than that of the east Asian mongoloid; he has a more prominent nose; and his skin pigmentation is in most cases darker. Slender in build, with dark eyes and a noticeable lack of body hair, he stands between 5 feet 2 inches and 5 feet 6 inches, although some groups – one for instance round Lake Atitlan in Guatemala – are small enough to be called pygmies. This is possibly a result of generations of inbreeding.

Highland Mexico was of all America the most densely settled area in the 16th century. Today there are an estimated 3,500,000 Indians in Mexico and Central America, a drastic decline from the pre-Conquest time: many died of imported diseases to which they had no resistance.

The Indians of Middle America cannot be regarded as distinct tribes as would, for example, the tribes of East Africa. The Indian communities are inhabitants of villages, groups of hamlets or rural regions who look towards a common civic or religious center, which houses the image of the saint who is patron to them all. People of one community tend to marry among themselves and are recognizable by their common peculiarities of language or dialect, costume, custom and the degree to which they have been hispanicized. Truly isolated communities such as the Lacandon are rare.

The large number of different Indian groupings in Mexico and Central America implies no political unity. But their way of life is remarkably uniform. Most Indians have similar religious beliefs, usually a mixture of Catholicism and their ancient religions. Most have the institutions of *compadrazgo* (imagined kinship ties whereby people can help and protect each other), the mayor domos (heads of large households) shamanism and the fiestas. (The shaman may be described as a priestly figure with powers to converse with supernatural beings, sometimes exercized in a state of drug-induced semi-trance.) They also tend to dress similarly and cultivate the Meso-American crop trilogy: maize, beans and squash (a vegetable of the pumpkin family). It is the variability in these institutions, with the linguistic and customary differences, that differentiates one community from another.

ACAXEE *Population:* 5,000. Language group: Taracahitan. Staple foods: beans, chilies. The Acaxee, now only a small group of Indians, live in the Mexican state of Durango. Formerly they occupied a large part of the Sierra Madre Occidental. They are farmers and fishermen, and drug fish with poison. Honey is a favorite food supplement. Their traditional craft is weaving. Their religion includes belief in gods of War and Creation. Once they practised cannibalism of fallen enemies and possibly infanticide. A favorite game is *pelota*, played with a ball made from tree sap, which may be hit with the buttocks and the right shoulder, but never touched by hand.

AGUATEC *Population:* 8,400. Language group: Mayan. Staple foods: maize, beans, squash. The Aguatec live in small isolated groups in the deep gorges and high peaks of the north-west highlands of Guatemala. Here they cultivate their farms with hoe, machete and digging stick, for the slopes are too steep to plow. They grow enough maize to export, and buy luxury commodities with the money; they also grow peaches, apples, potatoes. Most women go barefoot in spite of the cold. They live in rectangular, one-roomed houses without windows, but mostly with sweat-baths attached.

AMUZGO *Population:* 13,000. Language group: Amuzgo. Staple foods: maize, beans, squash. The Amuzgo live in rugged but verdant hills in south-east Guerrero state in Mexico, where they cultivate chilies, tomatoes, coffee, cocoa, rice and tobacco – and sugar-cane as their chief cash crop. Their larger villages are built in compact grid patterns, but many still live in dispersed homesteads. Their houses are round, single-roomed and thatched. The Amuzgo make animal offerings to the Earth and Rain.

AZTEC: Though the central Mexican Highlands were the heart of the Aztec empire, when the Spanish conqueror Cortés arrived in 1519, the empire collected tribute from states as far south as Guatemala and as far north as the Panuco River. The empire was soon destroyed by the Spaniards. The Huichol, Cora and Nahuatl are the chief Indian groups descended from the Aztec.

BLACK CARIBS *Population:* 30,000. Racially the Black Caribs are predominantly African, and culturally, Indian. They live scattered along the coast of the Gulf of Honduras, in Honduras, British Honduras and Guatemala. They came to the mainland of Central America from the Caribbean islands where they once were slaves. They live mainly by fishing and small scale horticulture. They have developed and maintained an identity very much their own.
(pages 102-105)

BORUCA *Population:* small. Language group: Chibchan. Staple foods: maize, beans, game, wild fruits and vegetables. The modern Boruca are probably a mixture of tribes indigenous to the Terraba plain of Costa Rica and western Panama. They were once important traders in salt with the forest Indians since they owned natural salt pans, but are now largely subsistence farmers and hunters.

BRIBRI *Population:* small. Language group: Chibchan. Staple foods: maize, beans, plantains. The few remaining Bribri live principally in the Caribbean lowlands of western Panama and Costa Rica. They practise slash-and-burn agriculture, chiefly for subsistence. They conquered the Terraba after a war at the beginning of the 19th century. They make a musical instrument of armadillo skin which is rubbed with a bean-like seed.

CAKCHIQUEL *Population:* 90,000. Language group: Mayan. Staple foods: maize, beans, squash. The Cakchiquel live in the mid-west highlands of Guatemala, subsistence-farming on the well-watered land, and going to the towns on market days and for festivals. They have retained much of their Indian culture, including the traditional craft of weaving. In the 16th century they allied themselves with the infamous Alvarado and his Spanish forces against their old enemies the Quiche.

CHATIÑO *Population:* 10,000. Language group: Zapotecan. Staple foods: maize, beans, squash. Chiefly concentrated in the Juquila district, the Chatiño live in the mountainous country of western Mexico from the Rio Grande to Zezantepec. They are

slash-and-burn agriculturalists who also grow coffee, which is replacing chocolate as their favorite beverage. They believe that while all wild animals are protected by spirit guardians, domestic animals are protected by saints. Chatiño shamans divine under the influence of narcotic mushrooms or the piule seed.

CHINANTEC *Population:* 61,000. Language group: Chinantecan. Staple foods: maize, beans. The Chinantec live in a small area called Chinantla on the forested north-facing slopes of the Oaxaca mountains in north Oaxaca state, Mexico. They have yucca and yam plantations, and breed pigs and fowl. They eat a lot of fresh-water fish; harpoons with detachable points are still used, as are dugout fishing canoes with stabilizers. The Chinantec girls still braid their hair in the traditional manner, coiling it with strips of cloth into a crown-like arrangement. Since traditional dress is no longer worn, the main craft of weaving is no longer important.

CHOCHO *Population:* 26,000. Language group: Popolocan. Staple food: maize. The Chocho live in the broken mountainous terrain of Mixteca Alta, north Oaxaca state, Mexico. Though rain is infrequent and torrential, they grow herbs and a wide variety of vegetables. They keep goats, chickens and turkeys, and their palm hats are considered masterpieces of art. By destroying the stalactite they regarded as a deity, Padre Abrego successfully evangelized the Chocho in the 19th century.

CHOL *Population:* 61,000. Language group: Mayan. Staple food: maize. The Chol live in Mexico in the mountains of northern Chiapas state near the border with Tabasco. Predominantly cultivators, the Chol supplement their staple diet with rice, potatoes, coffee, sugar-cane and vegetables, as well as by raising pigs and hunting. They live mostly in palm-roofed huts. The town of Tila is a religious center of great prestige in the south-east Mexico.

CHONTAL *Population:* 21,000. Language group: Mayan. Staple food: maize. The Chontal live in Chontalpa on the coast of Tabasco, Mexico. Besides maize, they grow beans, squash, peppers and sweet potatoes on

137

the fertile grasslands. They also eat fish and turtles caught in the sea. Their houses are rectangular with palm roofs and wooden walls. In the 16th century the Chontal were prosperous and used highly-valued cocoa as money. The straw-hat industry is now their most important enterprise.

CHORTI *Population:* 50,000. Language group: Mayan. Staple foods: maize, black beans. The Chorti live in the mountains on the Guatemala-Honduras border, chiefly in the municipios of La Union-Jacotan, San Juan, San Juan Hermita, Olapa and Copan. They are farmers and merchants. They sell their pottery and material woven by the Chorti women. Despite frequent contact with the *ladino* towns, these men from the hills retain much of their Indian tradition: they have never used their expensive market building erected over 50 years ago – they prefer the open plaza.

CHUH *Population:* 10,800. Language group: Mayan. Staple foods: maize, beans, squash. The Chuh live in the north-west highlands of Guatemala, in the northernmost range of mountains called the Chuchmatan. They grow maize as a cash crop, but also peaches, apples, and potatoes. They use the hoe, bushknife and digging stick as the slopes are too steep to plow.

COCOPA *Population:* 200. Language group: Hokan. Staple foods: wild fruit and maize. Once the Cocopa were a large tribe living in the Mexican state of Baja California. The few survivors now live in poverty around San Luis in Sonora state. Most live on reservations and are either wage laborers or small scale ranchers. They supplement their diet by hunting deer and rabbits and collecting wild foods. Most Cocopa have resisted Catholicism and retain their own beliefs in witchcraft and ghosts.

CORA *Population:* 7,000. Language group: Aztecoidan. Staple food: maize. The Cora live in the Sierra Madre Occidental mountain range in the Mexican states of Jalisco and Nayarit. They cultivate beans, squash, chilies and tomatoes, and also eat beef, venison and fish. Close relatives of the Huichol, they live in stone or wattle and daub houses in compact villages. In the late 1920's the Cora fought first for, then against, the 'Cristeros,' who protested against the government's rigorous policy towards ecclesiastical organizations.

CUICATEC *Population:* 9,000. Language group: Mixtecan. Staple foods: corn, beans, squash. In the southern Mexican highlands, the land of the Cuicatec falls away abruptly to the Rio Santo Domingo. These farmers supplement their staple crops with chilies, coffee and cocoa, as well as by keeping turkeys, chickens, pigs and cattle. They adhere to old food customs, eating locusts, worms, toasted ants and tobacco ashes. Little remains of their once-flourishing textile industry. Local religious beliefs and superstitions focus on Señor del Cerro (Lord of the Hill), the only supernatural being that comes close to being a specific deity.

CUITLATEC *Population:* 50,000. Language group: unclassified-extinct. Staple food: maize. Most of the Cuitlatec live in several towns on the Rio Balsas in the Mexican state of Guerrero. These excellent farmers cultivate the hill slopes with sesame, beans, corn, chilies and squash. They make rope, sacking and bamboo beds and specialize in carpentry and leatherwork. Formerly new-born children were taken to the Rock of Enchantment to acquire 'virtue'.

CUNA *Population:* small. Language group: Chibchan. Staple foods: bananas, corn, yams, rice, sweet manioc. One group of Cuna live around the headwaters of the rivers on the Pacific coast of Panama. Another group lives on the San Blas islands off Panama's Caribbean coast. As well as their slash-and-burn agriculture, fishing is important to their economy. They fish with nets, spears, bows and arrows, and harpoons (which they probably learned to use from immigrant negroes). They live in compact villages in rows of houses. Mainland Cuna have retained a greater degree of tribal identity than their fellows on the islands. Some of their shamans specialize in curing whole villages of epidemics. **(pages 114-121)**

GUAYMI *Population:* small. Language group: Chibchan. Staple foods: rice, maize, beans, plantains, pigeon peas. The Guaymi live in Costa Rica in Central America. The northern group live in tropical forest, the southern on the Pacific uplands. These slash-and-burn farmers also hunt, fish and collect wild foods. A few of the forest peoples hunt with a blow-gun using clay pellets. Some Indians keep cattle and horses, introduced in about 1900. Since the introduction of ranching, local laws about range areas, inheritance and cattle-stealing have evolved.

HUASTEC *Population:* 57,000. Language group: Mayan. Staple food: corn. The Huastec now live in the east coast Mexican state of Veracruz. Prior to the Spanish Conquest, they lorded over a vast area, from the Sierra Madre in the west to the Gulf of Mexico in the east. They grow coffee and keep pigs, dogs, cats, turkeys, chickens, and donkeys and use many of their old tools: digging stick, pestle, harpoon, and back-strap loom for weaving. They live in one-roomed houses scattered around the *municipios.*

HUAVE *Population:* 8,000. Language group: Huavean. Staple foods: fish, maize, beans, chilies, sweet potatoes. The Huave live in the Mexican state of Chiapas on the Pacific coast of the isthmus of Tehuantepec. It is an area of salt water lagoons, mangrove swamps and forests, and inland of grass and desert scrub. The Huave have a varied economic life because of their changing terrain. Fishing is the most important industry and the one that

IXIL *Population:* 25,000. Language group: Mayan. Staple foods: maize, beans, squash. The Ixil live in Guatemala, in the north-west highlands in the Ixcan valley. They are members of the Mam sub-group of Mayan speakers. Their cash crop is maize, but potatoes, peaches and apples are grown as well. They live in one-roomed stone houses, scattered over their farms. They are nominally Catholics but have their own local deities. The most important of these are called the 'owners of the mountains'.

JACALTEC *Population:* 13,500. Language group: Mayan. Staple foods: maize, beans, squash. The Jacaltec live in Guatemala in the north-west highlands on the western slopes of Chuchmatan highlands and in the low-lying valley along the Mexican border. They are members of the Kanhobal sub-group of Mayan-speakers. They are excellent farmers, whose cash crop is maize. They also grow apples, peaches and potatoes. They cultivate with hoes, machetes and digging sticks for the slopes are too steep to use a plow. A local movement known as the Cult of the Cross dominates their religious life.

JICAQUE *Population:* small. Language group: Jicaquean-Hokan. Staple foods: bitter manioc, wild foods. The few remaining

Jicaque Indians live in the eastern Caribbean lowlands of Honduras. In this flat, hot, humid region of rain forests and occasional swamps they practise slash-and-burn agriculture. They keep pigs, sheep, goats, cattle and horses, and grow maize as an export crop since they rarely eat it themselves. Traditional crafts include pottery, weaving and basketry.

KANHOBAL *Population:* 42,000. Language group: Mayan. Staple foods: maize, beans and squash. The Kanhobal live in the north-west highlands of Guatemala, in the central Cuchumatan mountains. It is an isolated region of high ridges and deep gorges. The Kanhobal are excellent farmers: they grow maize as a cash crop and also apples, peaches and potatoes. They cultivate with hoe, bushknife and digging stick as the slopes are too steep to plow. The most important of local beliefs is the Cult of the Cross. The crosses stand in front of the town churches and are sometimes built to a height of 70 feet. They are said to relate to an important date in the old Maya calendar.

KEKCHI *Population:* 178,000. Language group: Mayan. Staple food: maize. The Kekchi live in the mountains of central Guatemala. In the days of the Conquest this was an area of strong resistance to the Spanish. It was known as the Tierra de Guerra. There is now a small group of Kekchi in British Honduras. They are farmers but they supplement their diet with fish caught in the mountain streams. Before and after planting there are elaborate sex taboos: at midnight the night before the planting in the hope of a good harvest, husband and wife simulate sexual intercourse in three corners of the hut; in the fourth corner they consummate the act. Although much of their life has been influenced by Catholicism other traditional beliefs also persist. The Kekchi god, Tzultacaj, lives in large caves in the mountains and lies in a hammock hung by snakes which he keeps to punish sinners: small bites for minor sins and terrible bites for major foes. When he dies a Kekchi's body is wrapped and furnished with all the things he will need for his journey to the afterlife.

yields a surplus. The rest of the economy runs at subsistence level. In the forests they can hunt and further inland they cultivate. A farming household consists of a one-roomed house, storage buildings and a courtyard. This is surrounded by a stake or thatch fence.

HUICHOL *Population:* 7,000. Language group: Aztecoidan. Staple foods: maize, beans, fish. The Huichol live in the rugged mountains of the Sierra Madre in the western Mexican states of Jalisco and Nayarit. Though most live in or near the towns, some still farm on outlying ranches. Huichol communities send parties each winter to the sacred peyote-producing region in San Luis Potosi. **(pages 60-67)**

ICHATEC *Population:* 1,500. Language group: Popolocan. Staple foods: maize, beans, squash. The Ichatec live in high, mountainous country in north Oaxaca state, Mexico. Besides their staples, these farmers also eat maguey – a fleshy plant of the agave family – madrona worms and honey. Their main craft is weaving palm hats. Depending on their wealth, the Ichatec live in stone houses with tiled roofs or in palm-roofed huts.

KILIWA *Population:* 50. Language group: Aztecoidan. Staple foods: beans, wild fruits. The few remaining members of the once numerous Kiliwa tribe live in the Mexican state of Baja California. They have sold most of their land to Mexican ranchers and often work on their ranches. Some live with their neighbors the Paipai. With pale skin and straight dark hair it is difficult to tell them from the *mestizos*. Their favorite pastimes are playing cards and gambling. They still dance some of their traditional line-dances. They are not Catholic, and their religion centers around witchcraft, ghosts and healing.

LACANDON *Population:* 200. Language group: Mayan. Staple foods: corn, beans, squash, tomatoes. There are two groups of Lacandon in Mexico: one between the Rio Santo Domingo and the Rio Santa Cruz; another along the Cedro and Lacanha rivers. Previously hunters and gatherers, the few remaining Lacandon are now subsistence farmers. Before planting, new houses are built in the centers of the corn fields. They hunt and fish to supplement their diet. Much of their traditional religion and ritual has been lost, though they adopted very little from other cultures until the 20th century, when they first came into contact with peaceful outsiders. **(pages 84-93)**

LENCA *Population:* small. Language group: Lencan (unclassified). Staple foods: wheat, maize, plantains. The Lenca live in the steep, rugged regions of northern El Salvador and eastern Honduras and have been largely absorbed into the *mestizo* population. To supplement farming the Lenca hunt and fish; they dam the rivers and put in strips of poisonous barbasco vine to stun and trap the fish. Lenca are polygynous.

MAM *Population:* 180,000. Language group: Mayan. Staple foods: maize, beans, squash, peppers. The Mam live in the isolated highlands of north-west Guatemala. Being isolated, they have retained more indigenous culture than any other group of Maya. On land too steep for ox and plow they farm with hoes, machetes, and steel-pointed digging sticks. Religion centers on the rituals connected with the growth of maize and the protection of their fields. They sell their surplus maize. Their houses are one-roomed but most have a sweat-bath attached. This is entered through a door just big enough to crawl through and inside there is a bench of wood. Steam is produced by pouring water over hot stones; it is believed to hold curing

powers. Mam farms are scattered over the hills. The Maya calendar which was central to the Indian religious system is remembered in part in most communities.

MAYA *Population:* 2,000,000. Language group: Mayan. Apart from the Quechuan-speaking peoples of Peru and Ecuador the Mayan-speakers are the largest surviving group of American Indians. They live in the Mexican states of Chiapas and Yucatan, in the Guatemalan highlands and British Honduras. The relatively few *mestizos* in the Maya area are mostly confined to Yucatan and are, in any case, Mayan-speakers. Despite the collapse of the Maya empire, the farming Indians of the mountains live much as they did generations ago. Mayan-speakers include the following sometimes vaguely-defined groups: Aguacatec, Cakchiquel, Chorti, Ixil, Jacaltec, Kanhobal, Kekchi, Pokoman, Pokonchi, Quiche, Chuh, Uspantec, Rabinal, Tzeltal, Mam, Lacandon, Tzotzil, Tojolabal, Tzutuhil, and Solomec.

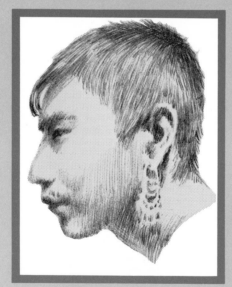

MAZATEC *Population:* 90,000. Language group: Popolocan. Staple foods: maize, chilies, squash. The Mazatec live in the Mexican state of Oaxaca on the borders of Puebla and Veracruz. They grow a limited range of crops on land which varies from sea-level plains to high mountains. Communal work takes on exceptional importance here and is performed with the compulsory help of officials and citizens alike.

MIXE *Population:* 50,000. Language group: Zoqueon. Staple foods: maize, beans, squash. The Mixe live in the eastern part of the Mexican state of Oaxaca. It is good hunting and fishing country as well as good farming land. The Mixe use narcotics to fish from the sluggish streams. They use the fire-hardened digging sticks and the Spanish plow for cultivating. Their houses are rectangular with one room and a grass-thatched roof. Their religion is similar to the ancient religion of the Aztec and the Maya.

MIXTEC *Population:* 175,000. Language group: Mixtecan. Staple foods: maize, beans, squash. The Mixtec live in parts of north and west Oaxaca and parts of Guerrero in Mexico. The Mixtec empire vied for power with the Zapotec. Its rulers maintained control by assassinating all possible usurpers. Where the land is poor, they weave palm for sale. They herd cattle and goats, and used to hunt and fish. They live either in villages or in scattered homesteads. Their stone houses are round or rectangular with one door, but no windows. Their religion is basically Catholic but old beliefs live on. The soul is seen as an entity which leaves the body at sleep and in death. The most important spirit is Tabayuku – the spirit of the hills. Local shamans cure by sacrifice or by the use of sweat-baths.

140

MOSQUITO *Population:* 15,000. Language group: Misumalpan. Staple foods: sweet manioc, wild foods. The few remaining members of the Mosquito (or Miskito) people live in the swampy eastern coastlands of Honduras and Nicaragua. (Their name is not derived from the insect nor *vice versa*.) These slash-and-burn farmers also keep pigs, sheep, goats, cattle and horses. Black paint is smeared over the men's bodies for decoration and protection from insects. In 1825 the whole tribe, under British guidance, was united under a 'king' who carried as insignia a staff and a gold or silver breast-plate.

NAHUA *Population:* 1,000,000. Language group: Aztecoidan. Staple foods: maize, chilies, beans. The Nahua, who speak Nahuatl, are Mexico's largest indigenous people. They live mainly in the states of San Luis Potosi, Hidalgo, Puebla, Guerrero and Veracruz. In Puebla they dress in the traditional way with pleated skirts of dark wool for women. They wear their hair in two braids tied at the back, and usually go barefoot. The men have a pudding-basin haircut and thong sandals. Farms are usually worked only by the family but the richer Nahua might hire some labor. They use wooden plows, hoes and machete and their cooking utensils include a simple pestle and mortar. Weaving is their oustanding craft.

OPATA *Population:* 2,000. Language group: Taracahitan. Staple food: maize. The Opata live in the north-west Mexican state of Sonora, inland around the sources of the Yaqui and Sonora rivers. Once far more numerous, they suffered from Apache Indian attacks as well as the Spanish invasion and quickly lost most of their native culture. They are now poor subsistence farmers. Since the early 1930s, their Opata dialect has become extinct.

OTOMI *Population:* 375,000. Language group: Otopamean. Staple foods: maize, beans, squash. The Otomi habitat is now restricted to the Central Plateau of Mexico, chiefly in the states of Hidalgo and Mexico. Not until the 19th century did the more recalcitrant groups of Otomi adopt *mestizo* farming techniques and assimilate *mestizo* culture, so losing much of their distinctiveness.

PAIPAI *Population:* 200. Language group: Hokan. Staple foods: beans, wild foods. There are now only a few of the Paipai left in the central highlands of the Mexican state of Baja California. They have a light colored skin and dark straight hair, and look like *mestizos*. They are extremely poor. Their only income is derived from small scale wage labor and ranching. They hunt rabbits and collect wild foods to keep from starving.

PAPAGO *Population:* 300. Language group: Piman. Staple food: maize. The few remaining members of the Papago tribe live in the Mexican state of Sonora, on the north-west coast. They live inland, touching on the border of Arizona USA. Many Papago migrated into Arizona as wage laborers. Those that remained in Mexico live on small ranches. The women make pottery. Their harvest fiesta is probably their only surviving native ceremony.

PAYA *Population:* small. Language group: unclassified – possibly Chibchan. Staple foods: bitter manioc, pineapples, chilies. The few remaining members of the Paya people live in the northern lowlands of Honduras and Nicaragua. They cultivate with simple tools: hoe, digging stick and machete, and they keep pigs, sheep, goats and cattle. They also raise opuntia – insects which produce the food-dye cochineal. Their crafts include pottery, weaving and basketry. They believe that God created mankind by sowing people like seeds on the earth.

PIMA *Population:* 1,400. Language group: Piman. Staple food: maize. The Pima live in the Mexican state of Sonora, in the hilly regions on the border of Chihuahua. There are now only a few left. Some are farmers although many work in the lumber mills. They drink an intoxicating liquor known as *mescal*.

POKOMAMES *Population:* 11,500. Language group: Mayan. Staple foods: maize, beans. The Pokomames live in the intensively cultivated eastern highlands of Guatemala. The more successful farmers manage to grow a surplus of maize for sale; profits depend on the market in Guatemala City. Charcoal burning, the responsibility of

men, and pottery, the responsibility of women, are the two main secondary industries. They have never adopted the Spanish symmetrical town planning as have the *mestizos* and many other Indian groups, but their houses increasingly have stone walls and sheet metal roofs. Guatemala City has become a strong attraction to the younger people of the community.

POPOLOCA *Population:* 18,500. Language group: Popolocan. Staple foods: maize, black beans. The Popoloca live in the state of southern Puebla in Mexico. In their semi-desert country trees grow only along the banks of rivers and creeks that cross the flat plain. They farm, but the shortage of water means that crops are often lost. In addition to their staples they grow avocados, oranges, lemons and papaya-fruit. The Popoloca live in towns and scattered homesteads. Traditional houses are wooden with grass or palm-thatched roofs. The more Hispanicized Indians live in stone houses with tile roofs. Their traditional crafts include palm weaving and pottery.

POPOLUCA *Population:* 15,000. Language group: Zoquean. Staple foods: maize, beans, squash. The Popoluca live on the Gulf of Mexico in southern Veracruz, the eastern end of the Tehuantepec isthmus. It is a fertile country, with oak and palm forests on the hills. The lowlands are savanna. The Popoluca are farmers who plant with a digging stick and hardly ever use the plow. Coffee, introduced to Mexico by Europeans, is their main export. The men hunt deer, rabbits, wild boar and game birds and take crayfish from the rivers after stupefying them with drugs. Their towns are symmetrical, in the Spanish pattern and result from Spanish attempts to gather the Indians together.

QUICHE *Population:* 540,000. Language group: Mayan. Staple foods: maize, beans, squash. The Quiche live in the mid-western highlands of Guatemala. Quiche women wear the traditional dress of colorful skirts, belts and blouses. The men wear highland dress: short black, embroidered trousers, black wool bolero jackets and cotton headcloths. They are farmers but tourist demand for their colorful handwoven fabrics makes weaving a thriving source of income. Pottery is less important but still a vital part of women's life. Most Quiche have two houses; one in the

141

state of Sonora. Women often paint their faces in colorful patterns. The men grow their hair long and wear a kilt of colored cloth over their trousers. The main occupation of the Seri is fishing. They live in little settlements along the coast, catching fish, turtles and shellfish. They have resisted Catholicism and are one of the few groups of Indians in Mexico to retain their traditional beliefs.
(pages 44-51)

SOLOMEC *Population:* 30,000. Language group: Mayan. Staple foods: maize, beans, squash. The Solomec live in the north-west highlands of Guatemala. It is an isolated area of high ridges and deep valleys and gorges. They are members of the Kanhobal sub-group of Mayan speakers. They live in one-roomed stone houses often with a sweat-bath attached.

SUMO *Population:* 4,000. Language group: Misumalpan. Staple foods: sweet manioc. The few remaining Sumo live in the northern lowlands of Honduras and Nicaragua. They cultivate by the slash-and-burn method, using simple implements. They live in small villages in houses with elaborately-carved central posts. Local crafts include pottery, weaving and basketry.

TARAHUMARA *Population:* 50,000. Language group: Taracahitian. Staple foods: corn, beans, squash and potatoes. The Tarahumara live in the mountains of south-west Chihuahua in Mexico. They call themselves the Raramuri: 'runners on foot'. Their economy is based on farming, but they also herd goats, sheep and cattle and hunt. They live in one-roomed log cabins. Their tools include steel axes, knives, hoes and chisels. In the 17th century the Tarahumara resisted the Spanish who wanted to mine for gold in the area. Pancho Villa's Mexican raiders roved the region in 1917 spreading disorder and disease.
(pages 52-59)

TARASCANS *Population:* 40,000. Language group: Tarascan. Staple foods: maize, beans and squash. The Tarascans now live in south-west Mexico, in the green mountains of Michoacan, from Lake Patzcuaro in the east to the Los Reyes railroad in the west. They

make their living by cattle husbandry for cash sale, by fishing, by exploiting the forest and by the sale of their handicrafts. Tarascan houses and grain-stores are either fenced or walled in. Towns are arranged symmetrically: the center of each town contains a church, a square and a town-hall.
(pages 76-83)

TEPECANO *Population:* 500. Language group: Piman. Staple food: *tortillas* made from corn. The few remaining members of the Tepecano tribe live in the mountainous southern part of the Mexican state of Durango. Most of them live in the town of Azqueltan, in the Bolaños canyon. They are closely related to the Southern Tepehuan, but are culturally more Hispanicized. It is thought that they were once Tepehuans who became isolated by the eastward expansion of the Huichol or by the Spanish advance northwards. Their language is nearly extinct.

TEPEHUAN, NORTHERN *Population:* 4,000. Language group: Piman. Staple foods: maize, beans, squash. The Northern Tepehuan live in the Mexican state of Chihuahua from the Rio Verde in the north to Guadalupe y Verde in the south. They cultivate small farms and keep some goats, chickens and turkeys. The women make pottery. They live in scattered villages and their houses are made of rough wooden planks. They store grain in lofts in their houses. Sickness and death are attributed to witchcraft; as among many central American Indians the second born of twins is killed.

TEPEHUAN, SOUTHERN *Population:* 2,500. Language group: Piman. Staple food: *tortillas* made from maize. The Southern Tepehuan live in the mountainous country in southern Durango state of Mexico, near Mezaguital. They are farmers and herders. They consider goat meat a great luxury and reserve beef for fiestas and funerals. Their traditional religion has absorbed an element of Christianity: their two principal deities are the sun-god Dios Padre and the moon-god Jesus Nazarano.

town and one in the farming areas. The towns are known as 'vacant towns', for empty houses stand around a square of church, market place and court house. The farmers move in on market days, at festivals and other ceremonial occasions.

RABINAL *Population:* 30,000. Language group: Mayan. Staple foods: maize, beans, squash. The Rabinal live in the mid-west highlands of Guatemala. It is a cool country of grasslands and trees, a stronghold of Indian settlement. They cultivate with hoe, machete and digging stick. Weaving is more important than pottery. Most houses have sweat-baths attached: they are small stone mounds, with a door just big enough to crawl through and are believed to be beneficial to the sick.

RAMA *Population:* 300. Language group: Chibchan. Staple foods: maize, beans, wild foods. Formerly much larger, the present principal Rama settlement is on Rama Quay in the Laguna de Bluefields. A few scattered settlements are also found between this island and Punta Gorda on the Caribbean coastlands of Nicaragua. They are slash-and-burn agriculturalists and hunters.

SERI *Population:* 300. Language group: Serian. Staple foods: fish, wild food. The Seri live on the coast of the north-west Mexican

TEQUISTLATEC *Population:* 11,000 (1940s). Language group: Tequistlatec. Staple foods: *tortillas,* made from maize, cucurbits (a plant of the gourd family), haricot beans and maguey (agave). They live in Mexico in the mountainous areas of Sierra Madre del Sur, south central Oaxaca. Agriculture is the basis of the Tequistlatec economy, but also important are animal husbandry and hunting. Their tools include fire-sharpened digging sticks and the machete. The men do most of the agricultural work; the women make baskets and pottery. Houses are usually of two rooms, each occupied by a separate family. Catholicism has had little influence. They believe in a plurality of some fifteen Gods, and have an elaborate mythology.

TIPAI *Population:* 100. Language group: Hokan. Staple foods: beans, wild foods. The few remaining members of the Tipai people live in the Mexican state of Baja California in the hills on the border of California USA. Many of them have crossed over into California as wage laborers. They supplement their basic diet by hunting deer, rabbits and collecting wild foods. Most of them live in reservations. They have resisted Catholicism and their indigenous religion centers on witchcraft, ghosts and healing by shamans, who obtain their power by the use of the poisonous Jimson weed.

TLAPANEC *Population:* 23,500 (1937). Language group: Supanecan. Staple foods: bananas, coffee, chilies, maize, sugar-cane and beans – although poorer members of the tribe cannot afford beans. The Tlapanec live in five different districts in the state of Guerrero in Mexico, but chiefly in the Merelos area. They are among the least known of the middle American Indians. They are excellent carpenters though they use the simplest tools: wedge, axe and chisel. Women weave and make pottery. The Tlapanec are settled in towns and live in small one-roomed dwellings. They have two principal gods – one male and one female – in addition to a number of impersonal gods. They are superstitious and practise magic. Fiestas are their main recreation and at these occasions they drink alcoholic *aquardiente* and *pulque*.

TOJOLABAL *Population:* 50,000. Language group: Mayan. Staple food: maize. The Tojolabal live in the municipios of Comitan las Margueritas, la Independencia and la Trinitaria, all of which are in the highland

Mexican state of Chiapas. Pig and chicken farming are important. The men do most of the heavy work while the women do all the housework and help with the harvest. In their scattered villages, called *rancherias*, they live in wattle and daub houses with high pitched thatched roofs. There are also out-buildings, animal shelters and corn storage bins. After harvest a man gives a fiesta for all those who have helped him. Caves are centers of worship particularly for rain. They attribute illness to witchcraft and bury their dead with their personal possessions.

TOTONAC *Population:* 90,000. Language group: Totonacan. Staple foods: maize and squash. They live in the states of Puebla and Veracruz in Mexico. Their land is varied, ranging from high rocky plateau to lowland. They grow crops and breed chicken and pigs. Their tools are of native origin, except in the highland where they cut timber with commercial saws. Their huts are rectangular and palm-thatched, with bamboo-pole walls. Many rites of their old religion remain; the present era began with the rising sun and will end with a flood. There are two types of fiesta: a private one, and a public church fiesta, where men drink *tepache* – fermented from juice of several fruits – and the women sherry and anise.

TRIQUE *Population:* 3,000. Language group: Mixtecan. Staple foods: corn and beans. The Trique live in Mexico in the mountains and forests of Oaxaca. They farm and hunt wild pigs, deer, doves, rabbits and squirrels. They also eat a species of spider, ants, frogs, beetles and grass-hoppers. The Trique live mostly in towns in crowded one-roomed houses. In the mountains they live in spacious ranches. The Trique have long been exploited by whites and *mestizos* and have a history of hostilities against them. In 1956 several soldiers were killed when federal airplanes bombed Trique settlements, and soldiers have since been permanently stationed in them.

TZELTAL *Population:* 49,000. Language group: Mayan. Staple food: maize. The Tzeltal live in the central part of the state of Chiapas, Mexico. The area is divided into three zones: gentle slopes and plains in the south, high peaks in the center, and lower peaks in the north. The Tzeltal clear small areas of land for their staple crops, abandoning them for new clearings every few years when the soil is exhausted – a system known as the *milpa*. Their supplementary crops are chilies, beans, corn and squash. Men look after the *milpa* while the women are responsible for the household and pottery production. Their tools include the axe, machete and hoe. All the tribal communities consist of a town center surrounded by a number of settlements called Parajes. They work periodically on the Pacific coast coffee plantations.
(pages 94-101)

TZOTZIL *Population:* 114,000. Language group: Mayan. Staple foods: maize, beans and squash. The Tzotzil (people of the bat) live in the Chiapas highlands in Mexico. Their land begins in the tropical lowlands, crosses the western sector of the mountain chain and drops down to the Grijalva river 150 km to the north. In addition to their agricultural economy they practise animal husbandry and use oxen and mules as beasts of burden. The men farm and the women weave and make cotton and woollen products. A typical Tzotzil house is of a single room that serves as a dormitory, kitchen, living room and storage space. The walls are made of cane poles and the roof is palm thatched.
(pages 94-101)

143

TZUTUHIL *Population:* 80,000. Language group: Mayan. Staple foods: maize, beans, squash. The Tzutuhil live in the mid-west highlands of Guatemala. Here Indians far outnumber the *mestizos* and Spanish people. They are good farmers who subsist easily in their fertile country. Most live on their farms but also have houses in the otherwise empty local towns where they go to sell in the market or to attend festivals. Nominally Catholic, they see illness as a weakness or a failure to observe prescribed behavior towards the supernatural spirits.

USPANTEC *Population:* 100,000. Language group: Mayan. Staple foods: maize, beans, squash. The Uspantec live in the cool, fertile mid-west highlands of Guatemala. They are part of the Quichean sub-group of the Mayan-speakers. Like the Tzutuhils, their towns – built for them by governments bent on centralization – are usually vacant, visited only for market and festivals. Their local crafts are weaving and pottery. Their beliefs are comparable to the Tzutuhil's.

YAQUI *Population:* 15,000. Language group: Taracahitian. Staple food: maize, beans and squash. Yaqui society formerly centered on 8 towns on the banks of the Yaqui River in Mexico. But today North Americans and Mexicans have moved in and diverted the river, leaving the Yaqui without their most important asset. So they are reduced to living by wage-labor. The tribal religion is essentially Jesuit. Occasionally they take two husbands or wives but never repeat the marriage ceremony. Although they accept the Roman Catholic ban on divorce they frequently exchange spouses. By their cult of the dead each family keeps a book which records the names of ancestors. They place this book on the altar at all ceremonies. A recent writer, Carlos Castaneda, describes in rich detail how he tried, through a Yaqui shaman called Don Juan, to meet 'Mescalito,' the awe-inspiring god of peyote.

ZAPOTEC *Population:* 300,000. Language group: Zapotecan. Staple foods: maize, squash, beans. The Zapotec live over a vast area of central Mexico. Most are farmers, and they are reputed to be commercially minded. Coffee is their chief export crop.

All population figures are approximate.

With no shortage of land, fields are cleared and used until the crops dwindle when new clearings are made. They fish and hunt to supplement their diet. Most Zapotec believe they were born from mountains, rocks and caves; that the first chief came from the sky as a bird; and that there is a hierarchy of gods which dominates the universe of which those who control the natural phenomena also control agriculture. At death, they place the body in a wooden box with food, a change of clothes and some water to help it on its journey to the afterlife. The isthmus Zapotec have a love for romantic music, passionate poetry and great speechmaking.

ZOQUE *Population:* 38,000. Language group: Zoquean. Staple foods: maize, beans and squash. They live on a belt of land in western Chiapas which stretches from Tuxtla Gutierrez to Tabasco. The country is less high and broken than that of the neighboring Mixe people, and in places it is fertile. As well as their staples, they grow pineapples, papaya-fruit, tomatoes and coffee. They also fish by stunning the fish with narcotics. Some people live in log cabins with tiled roofs, but most have grass-thatched huts. They have a religion similar to that of the Mixe which identifies the pulse with the soul: a weak pulse means a fading soul. The hallucinogenic mushroom (from which mescalin is produced) has for them a religious significance.